JOSSEY-BASS

Janice VanCleave's

Great Science Project Ideas from Real Kids

Janice VanCleave

South Huntington Pub. Lib.
145 Pidgeon Hill Rd.
Huntington Sta., N.Y. 11746

John Wiley & Sons, Inc.

This book is printed on acid-free paper. ∞

Copyright © 2007 by Janice VanCleave. All rights reserved.

Illustrations © 2007 by Laurie Hamilton. All rights reserved.

Published by Jossey-Bass
A Wiley Imprint
989 Market Street, San Francisco, CA 94103-1741

Design and composition by Navta Associates, Inc.

No part of this publication may be reproduced, stored in a retrieval system, or transmitted in any form or by any means, electronic, mechanical, photocopying, recording, scanning, or otherwise, except as permitted under Section 107 or 108 of the 1976 United States Copyright Act, without either the prior written permission of the Publisher, or authorization through payment of the appropriate per-copy fee to the Copyright Clearance Center, Inc., 222 Rosewood Drive, Danvers, MA 01923, 978-750-8400, fax 978-646-8600, or on the Web at www.copyright.com. Requests to the Publisher for permission should be addressed to the Permissions Department, John Wiley & Sons, Inc., 111 River Street, Hoboken, NJ 07030, 201-748-6011, fax 201-748-6008, or online at http://www.wiley.com/go/permissions.

The publisher and the author have made every reasonable effort to ensure that the experiments and activities in the book are safe when conducted as instructed but assume no responsibility for any damage caused or sustained while performing the experiments or activities in this book. Parents, guardians, and/or teachers should supervise young readers who undertake the experiments and activities in this book.

Permission is given for individual classroom teachers to reproduce the pages and illustrations for classroom use. Reproduction of these materials for an entire school system is strictly forbidden.

Jossey-Bass books and products are available through most bookstores. To contact Jossey-Bass directly call our Customer Care Department within the U.S. at 800-956-7739, outside the U.S. at 317-572-3986, or fax 317-572-4002.

Jossey-Bass also publishes its books in a variety of electronic formats. Some content that appears in print may not be available in electronic books.

Library of Congress Cataloging-in-Publication Data

VanCleave, Janice Pratt.
  [Great science project ideas from real kids]
  Janice VanCleave's great science project ideas from real kids / Janice VanCleave.
    p. cm.
  Includes index.
  ISBN-13 978-0-471-47204-9 (pbk. : alk. paper)
  ISBN-10 0-471-47204-2 (pbk. : alk. paper)
 1. Science projects—Juvenile literature. 2. Science—Experiments—Juvenile literature.
I. Title: Great science projects ideas from real kids. II. Title.
  Q182.3.V354 2006
  507'.8—dc22
                                        2005031899

Printed in the United States of America
first edition

Dedication

It is with pleasure that I dedicate this book to three people whose help in writing this book was invaluable: Matt LoDolce, Diane M. Flynn, and my daughter, Ginger Russell. Matt is not just one of the real kids who contributed science project ideas, but he also introduced me to his science teacher, Diane M. Flynn. Diane and her students, who contributed ideas, have been a joy to work with. Working with Ginger, who is my daughter, was an extra-special pleasure. She assisted in collecting ideas from kids in homeschool organizations and in public schools.

Contents

Acknowledgments   vii

Introduction   1

Part I   SCIENCE PROJECTS STEP-BY-STEP

Chapter 1   Keep a Log Book   7
Chapter 2   Select a Category   9
Chapter 3   Do Topic Research   12
Chapter 4   Do Project Research   14
Chapter 5   Find a Project Problem   17
Chapter 6   Come Up with a Project Hypothesis   18
Chapter 7   Design a Project Experiment   19
Chapter 8   Collect Raw Data   21
Chapter 9   Create Your Project Summaries   25
Chapter 10   Design Your Project Display   30
Chapter 11   Prepare an Oral Presentation and Plan for Your Evaluation   33

Part II   40 SAMPLE PROJECTS

Project 1   What Effect Does the Physical Form of a Fertilizer Have on Plant Growth?   36
Project 2   What Effect Does Talcum Powder Have as an Insecticide?   38
Project 3   How Effective Are Sun Shadows for Telling Time?   40
Project 4   How Does Earth's Rotation Affect the Position of the "Man in the Moon"?   42
Project 5   What Effect Does a Glucose Solution Have on the Longevity of Cut Flowers?   44
Project 6   What Effect Does the Color of Light Have on Phototropism?   46
Project 7   What Effect Does the Position of Artificial Light Have on Plant Growth?   48
Project 8   How Does Exposure Time to Microwaves Affect Seed Germination?   50
Project 9   What Effect Does the Size of a Plant's Leaves Have on the Plant's Transpiration Rate?   52
Project 10   How Do Seasonal Color Changes in the Environment Affect Camouflage in Animals?   54
Project 11   How Does the Amount of Water in a Gel Affect Its Flexibility?   56
Project 12   What Effect Does the Type of Flour Have on the Ability of Calcium Propionate to Inhibit Bread Mold?   58

Project 13	What Effect Does Light Have on the Rate of Planaria Regeneration?	60
Project 14	What Effect Does Regular Physical Exercise Have on the Lungs' Vital Capacity?	62
Project 15	What Effect Does Gender Have on the Stroop Test Color Recognition Response Time?	64
Project 16	How Does the Volume of Background Music Affect Short-Term Memory?	66
Project 17	How Does Color Intensity Affect the Perceived Sweetness of Food?	68
Project 18	What Effect Does the Type of Video Game Have on Blood Pressure?	70
Project 19	What Effect Does Surface Area Have on the Evaporation Rate of Water?	72
Project 20	What Effect Does Temperature Have on the Amount of Solute Needed to Prepare a Saturated Solution?	74
Project 21	What Effect Does Surface Texture Have on Growing Crystals?	76
Project 22	What Effect Does Temperature Have on the Thickness of Ketchup?	78
Project 23	What Effect Does the pH of Food Have on Preventing Tarnish on Copper Pots?	80
Project 24	What Effect Does the Concentration of a Mordant Have on the Colorfastness of a Natural Dye?	82
Project 25	How Effective Are Homemade Barometers in Predicting Weather?	84
Project 26	What Effect Does Humidity Have on Condensation Rate?	86
Project 27	How Does Evaporation Affect the Salinity of Ocean Water?	88
Project 28	What Effect Does the Type of Ground Cover Have on the Rate of Soil Erosion?	90
Project 29	How Does the Texture of Paper Affect Its Printing Quality?	92
Project 30	What Type of Container Increases the Shelf Life of Bread?	94
Project 31	How Does the Degree of Stretching Affect the Ability of Plastic Food Wraps to Keep Foods Fresh?	96
Project 32	What Effect Does Triangle Size Have on the Strength of a Truss Bridge?	98
Project 33	How Steady Is the Moon's Angular Speed from One Day to the Next?	100
Project 34	How Does the Ratio of Two Dyes in a Mixture Affect Its Color?	102
Project 35	How Does a Refrigerant's Surface Area Affect How Well It Cools?	104
Project 36	What Effect Does Salt Concentration Have on the Specific Heat of an Aqueous Salt Solution?	106
Project 37	What Effect Does the Time of Day Have on Passive Solar Heating?	108
Project 38	How Does the Size of a Vibrating Surface Affect the Pitch of Its Sound?	110
Project 39	How Does Density Affect the Buoyancy of Objects?	112
Project 40	How Does Mass Affect the Period of a Pendulum?	114
Appendix A	100 Project Ideas	117
Appendix B	Science Project and Reference Books	122
	Glossary	126
	Index	133

Acknowledgments

I wish to express my appreciation to these science specialists for their valuable assistance in providing information and/or finding it for me: Dr. Ben Doughty, Robert Fanick, Holly Harris, and Dr. Tineke Sexton. Dr. Doughty is the head of the department of physics at Texas A&M University—Commerce in Commerce, Texas. Mr. Fanick is a chemist at Southwest Research Institute in San Antonio, Texas. Ms. Harris is a chemistry instructor and science fair director at China Spring High School—China Spring, Texas. Dr. Sexton is an instructor of biology and microbiology at Houston Community College Northwest—Houston, Texas. The valuable information these special scientists have provided me has made this book even more understandable and fun.

A special note of gratitude goes to James H. Hunderfund, Ed.D., superintendent of schools; Pamela J. Travis-Moore, principal; and James Engeldrum, science chairperson, of Commack Middle School. Because of the approval and support of these supervisors, young scientists at the school, under the direction of teachers Diane M. Flynn, Loni Mui, and Ellen M. Vlachos, contributed ideas and input for the science projects that appear in Part II, "40 Sample Projects." These scientists are Danny Abrams, Amanda Accardi, Robert Ali, Louis Arens, Scott Aronin, Sam Austin, Jesse Badash, Andrew Benin, Tara Bereche, Rachel Bloom, Randi Bloom, Matthew Brendel, Ryan William Brown, Chris Caccamo, Tia Canonico, John Paul Carollo, Jenna Cecchini, Naomi Chalfin, Samson Cheung, Jennifer Ciampi, Christine Cirabisi, Melissa Coates, Alyssa Cohen, Laura Coiro, Sarah Corey, Vincent Daigger, Alana Davacino, Suzy Ezzat, Nicole Fieger, Julie Fink, Brandon Fishman, Colleen Fitzsimons, Gianna Flora, Kate Foley, Jen Fox, Megan Ganzenmuller, Amy Grabina, John Halloran, Michael Iadevaia, Saba Javadi, Rosemary Kalonaros, Valerie Kamen, Jamie Keller, Kevin Kim, Lisa Kim, Matthew J. Kim, Savina Kim, David Klein, Melissa Kowalski, Joshua Krongelb, Jillian Lecarie, Jaclyn Leiser, Julia Leone, Arielle Lewen, Alexandra Lionetti, Alec Litrel, Kaelyn Lynch, Taylor Macy, Kylan Maguire, Brittany Manchio, Taylor Manoussos, Ian Ross Marquit, Philip Mauser, Steven Mauser, Marissa McCort, Alana Martz, Spencer D. Mason, Frank Mendyk, Kayla Miklas, Bryan Moore, Declan Morgan, David Murphy, Jordan Nissen, Bryan D. Noonan, Greg Oh, Daniel O'Leary, Rachel Orfinger, Stephanie Pennetti, Jennifer Phelan, Erica Portnoy, GemmaRose Raggozine, Arpon Raskit, Anthony V. Riccio, Ayden Rosenberg, Lauren Rubenstein, Lauren Scanlan, Daniel E. Scholem, Grant D. Schum, Lauren Shannon, Arielle Simner, Danielle Simone, Hunter Smith, Allison Smithwick, Brian Somsook, Brandon A. Smail, Andrew Spahn, Evan Sunshine, Katherine Treubig, Suraj Uttam, Frank Walsh, Brian Ward, Marni Wasserman, Michael Weber, Daniel Weissman, Chris Wenz, John Werst, Ashlyn Wiebalck, Aaron Wilson, Daniel Zaklis, Christopher M. Zambito, Alice Zhou.

I also want to express my thanks to the following young scientists who also contributed ideas and input for the science projects: Olivia Anderson; Jonna Butcher; Jared, Rachel, and Sara Cathey; James Alexander and McKayla Lynsie Conner; Catherine E. and Zachary N. C. Daunis; Drake Edward; Connor Fields; Evan Filion; Britney Fleming; Emily Frazier; Annie Frey; Tyler Halpern; Chris Holifield; Clay Hooper; Connor Janeski; Lindsey Lewis; Sebastian Mead; Ben and Hank Osborne; Lea Roldan; Lacey Russell; Benjamin, Sarah, and Rebecca Skrabanek; Taylor Stephens; David VanCleave; Donald VanVelzen; Alessia Vettese; Easton and Weston Walker; Megan Witcher; Jacob Stephen Wood; and Sarah Yount.

Introduction

This book presents fun science facts and projects for young people. All of the projects are based on ideas from real kids like you. We hope they'll give you a sense of what you can do for your own unique science project.

Science is a system of knowledge about the nature of things in the universe. It is the result of observing, questioning, and experimenting to test ideas. A **science project** is an investigation designed to find the answer to one specific science question or purpose called a **project problem**.

Many science projects are done for a contest called a **science fair** (an organized contest in which science projects are compared and judged based on predetermined criteria). You must follow certain rules in preparing your project. You'll learn about a lot of those rules in the first part of this book, which takes you step-by-step through the process for creating a great project.

Developing a science fair project is like being a detective. It requires that you plan well, carefully collect information, analyze the information, and share your findings. Preparing and presenting a science project can be a fun and rewarding experience, but trying to develop the project and/or assemble the display at the last minute usually results in frustration.

Begin your project with curiosity and a desire to learn something new. Then proceed with a goal and determination to solve the problem. Even if your project doesn't turn out exactly as you planned, it is likely that your scientific quest will end with some interesting discoveries.

How to Use This Book

This book will give you guidance in developing your project from start to finish, including information and techniques on how to design and present a project. Before you start your project, read all of part I. It contains 11 chapters, each with key steps to follow for science fair success.

1. *Keep a log book.* A **log book** is a science diary or journal, which is a written record of your project from start to finish. This chapter describes what kind of things go into a log book and how best to organize it.

2. *Select a category.* A **project category** is a group of related science topics. This chapter provides a list of some of the common categories used in science fairs. Check with your teacher for other possible categories in your fair. This list can be used to help select your project topic, and it should be used to identify the category that best describes your project. Judges base their evaluation of the content of your project on the category in which you enter it. For example, an earth science project incorrectly entered in the chemistry category most likely will receive a lower rating.

3. *Do topic research.* Selecting a topic is often considered the hardest part of a

science fair project. The research suggested in this chapter will help make choosing a topic more enjoyable. **Research** is the process of collecting information. **Topic research** is research done with the objective of selecting a project topic.

4. *Do project research.* **Project research** is an in-depth study of the project topic, with the objective of identifying these parts of the project: the problem, the hypothesis, and the experiment. This research should involve more than just reading printed materials. It should include interviews with people who are knowledgeable about the topic as well as **exploratory experiments** (experiments in which the results are part of the project research). This chapter provides suggestions and directions for gathering project research.

5. *Find a project problem.* The project problem is a scientific question to be solved or a purpose statement to be tested. This chapter provides information and examples of different kinds of project problems.

6. *Come up with a project hypothesis.* A **project hypothesis** is a prediction of the solution to a project problem, based on knowledge and research. This chapter provides examples of hypotheses for different kinds of projects.

7. *Design a project experiment.* A **project experiment** is an experiment that tests a project hypothesis. This chapter is key to the success of your project, and the information in this chapter will help you create the right kind of experiment for your particular type of project.

8. *Collect raw data.* **Data** are recorded collections of information. **Raw data** are experimental results from the project experiment. This chapter provides ways to organize and display data, including examples of different types of graphs.

9. *Create your project summaries.* **Project summaries** include an abstract and a report based on data from your log book. This chapter includes information on how to prepare a **project abstract** (a brief overview of a scientific project) and a **project report** (a written report of an entire project from start to finish).

10. *Design your project display.* In addition to your project summaries, a **project display** is your way of communicating to others what you did and what you learned. It's important that you use the space you've been given wisely to represent your project in the best way possible. This chapter provides ideas for designing a project display that will not only catch the eye of observers but will hold their attention.

11. *Prepare an oral presentation and plan for your evaluation.* Although your presentation and evaluation come at the end of the process, you should be thinking about them throughout the development of the project. It is important to consider how you will be evaluated so that your project entry meets the necessary criteria. This chapter helps to prepare you for the judging process and gives hints of what to expect at the fair. Your teacher can provide more specific information.

Part II provides examples of project research and ideas for planning and developing projects for 40 science fair topics. All of the projects are based on ideas from real kids in each of the eight curricula: agriculture, astronomy, biology, chemistry, earth science, engineering, mathematics, and physics.

The projects are not complete but are suggestions for you to use in developing your own project. Concepts covered in different projects may overlap, so review the ideas in two or three projects on related topics to get a wide range of ideas.

Each project starts with a problem followed by research information about the topic being investigated. Then each project gives clues for an experiment to answer the problem, including suggestions for a **control** (an experiment used for comparison) and the **variables** (things that can change). The three types of variables are the **independent variable** (the part of an experiment that is purposely changed), the **dependent variable** (the part of an experiment that changes due to changes in the independent variable), and the **controlled variables** (parts of an experiment that could change but are kept constant). Each project also includes a list of other questions related to the topic that can be explored.

Appendix A provides a list of 100 project problems in agriculture, astronomy, biology, chemistry, earth science, engineering, mathematics, and physics. This list, which includes independent and dependent variables, gives you more ideas that may help you select a topic for your project.

The appendix provides a list of reference and project books where you can find more information on the topic of each project.

The fun of a science fair project lies in exploring a topic in which you're interested, finding and recording information, planning the project experiment, organizing the data, and reaching a conclusion. The objective of a science fair project is for you to make your own discoveries. Whether you win a ribbon at the fair or not, all science fair participants who do their best earn the prize of being first-place scientists. This is your opportunity to be a winner! Let's get started.

Part I

Science Projects Step-by-Step

Chapter 1

Keep a Log Book

The first step you must do for a science fair project is create a log book (a science diary), which is a written record showing the progression of your project from start to finish. The log book contains your notes and doesn't have to be in report form. Your log book is usually a part of your science fair display, so it may be included in the judging of your project.

Here are some handy tips for constructing your log book:

- Use a binder or a folder so that pages can be organized.
- Use labeled and tabbed sections to show parts of the study. (This chapter gives suggestions for tabs.)
- Date all entries.
- Include all experimental observations in order by date, and include the time if appropriate.
- Record your thoughts and questions during the entire study.
- Make the log book as neat, organized, and user-friendly as possible.
- Number each page after completing the log book.
- Include a table of contents that lists the first page for each part.

Don't rewrite any of the entries to make them look neater. If you do this, you might accidentally add or delete information. Stains on the pages don't matter.

Sections for the log book can include:
1. **Project rules and regulations.** This section contains all printed information provided by your teacher that is related to the project, including rules and deadlines for each step of the project.
2. **A planning calendar.** Make a list of all the project steps and the dates when you plan to complete each one. This will help you plan your time so that you use it wisely. In creating the calendar, you should schedule enough time so that you are finished by the date the final project is due. The calendar might include the following deadlines:

Steps	Deadline Date
1. Set up log book	
2. Project topic chosen	
3. Project research done	
4. Project question decided	
5. Project hypothesis determined	
6. Project experiment designed	
7. Project experiment performed	
8. Study and record results	
9. Project report done	
10. Project display done	
11. Project due	

3. **Project topic research.** Start by listing the categories in which you are interested. Then list the topics in each category that you might want to investigate. Narrow down this list to specific topics. Include information about all the resources that you used—magazines,

books, and so on—as you searched for a topic. Chapter 3 provides information about doing topic research.
4. **Project research.** This is research to help you understand the project topic, express a problem, propose a hypothesis, and design a project experiment. Project research is the process of collecting information from knowledgeable sources such as books, magazines, software, librarians, teachers, parents, scientists, or other professionals. It is also data collected from exploratory experiments. Be sure to give credit where credit is due, and record all information, data, and sources in your log book.
5. **The project problem.** Record all ideas about your project problem. If you have more than one idea or if the problem is revised, indicate the final decision.
6. **The project hypothesis.** Keep a record of all hypothesis ideas. Indicate the final hypothesis.
7. **The project experiment.** This experiment is designed to test your hypothesis. It should have measurable results. Keep a list of all your materials and record your step-by-step procedure.
8. **The project data.** These are the observations and measured results obtained from the project experiment. This information could be recorded in a table or a graph.
9. **The project summaries.** This section includes your analysis of the data for the **project abstract** (a brief overview of the project) and the **project report** (a written record of your entire project from start to finish). As with other parts of your log book, this section should contain all your work to show how different summaries were edited and revised.
10. **The project display.** Keep all information about the display in this section. It should include all drawings, tables, and graphs you consider for the display.
11. **The project presentation and evaluation.** Written copies of oral presentations should be kept in this section. Also include information about rules for presentations, such as length of time, as well as information about how the project will be judged.

Chapter 2

Select a Category

The second step of the project is to study the project categories. This chapter has a list of common categories with brief descriptions, but ask your teacher for a list of categories for your fair. It is important that you enter your project in the correct category. Since science fair judges are required to judge the content of each project based on the category in which it is entered, you could be seriously penalized if you entered your project in the wrong category.

Some topics can be correctly placed in more than one category; for example, the structure of plants could be in botany or anatomy. If you are in doubt about the category of your project, find the topic in a textbook to see under which category it is listed. Each of the 40 projects in Part II are marked with the category in which they could be entered. The categories listed here can be used in identifying a project topic, as discussed in Chapter 4, as well as determining the category of the topic you choose:

- **Agriculture.** The science that deals with farming concerns.
  1. **Fertilizer.** The study of **nutrients** (nourishing materials necessary for life) added to the soil to increase plant production.
  2. **Insect pest management.** The study of methods of controlling insects that affect crop production as well as the health of farm animals.
- **Astronomy.** The study of **celestial bodies** (natural objects in the sky such as stars, moons, suns, and planets).
  1. **Celestial motion.** The study of the motion of celestial bodies.
  2. **Earth's natural satellite.** The study of Earth's Moon—Earth's **natural satellite**, which is one celestial body that moves in a circular path about another.
  3. **Stellar science.** The study of stars, including their composition, magnitude, classification, structure, and groupings.
- **Biology.** The study of living things.
  1. **Botany.** The study of plants and plant life. Subtopics include:
     a. **Anatomy.** The study of the structure of plants, such as seeds and the vascular system.
     b. **Behavior.** The study of actions that alter the relationship between a plant and its environment, such as plant **tropism**, which is the movement of an organism in response to a **stimulus** (something that temporarily excites or quickens a response in organisms), such as **phototropism** (movement in response to light) or **geotropism** (movement in response to gravity).
     c. **Physiology.** The study of life processes of plants, including germination, transpiration, transportation of nutrients, and plant growth.
  2. **Ecology.** The study of relationships of living things to other living things and to their environment.
  3. **Food science.** The study of food, including the causes of food deterioration and the nature of food, such as nutritional value.

4. **Microbiology.** The study of **microscopic organisms** (organisms that you need a microscope to see because they are so small).
5. **Reproduction.** The study of **reproduction** (the process of producing a new organism), either **sexual** (involving two parents) or **asexual** (involving only one parent).
6. **Zoology.** The study of animals and animal life. Subtopics may include:
   a. **Anatomy.** The study of the structure and function of animal body parts, including vision, taste, and hearing.
   b. **Behavior.** The study of the actions and reactions of humans and animals using observational and experimental methods.
   c. **Physiology.** The study of the life processes of animals, including respiration, circulation, the nervous system, and metabolism.
- **Chemistry.** The study of what substances are made of and how they change and combine.
  1. **Chemical changes.** The study of the changes made when the particles of one or more substances combine or break apart and recombine in a new way to produce one or more different substances. A **chemical** is any substance with a definite composition made of one or more elements. **Elements** are substances made of one kind of **atom** (the building blocks of elements).
  2. **Physical changes.** The study of the physical properties of substances that are physically changed. A change may occur in the appearance of matter, but its properties and makeup remain the same. Subtopics may include:
     a. **Crystallography.** The study of the formation of crystals as well as the crystals themselves.
     b. **Mixtures.** A combination of two or more substances. The study of the properties of the whole and/or parts of a **homogeneous mixture** (a mixture that has the same composition throughout) and a **heterogeneous mixture** (a mixture that does not have the same composition throughout.
     c. **States of matter.** A study of how the particles of a substance change to form three common states on Earth: gas, liquid, and solid.
- **Earth science.** The study of the parts of Earth: the **atmosphere** (the gas layer surrounding Earth), the **lithosphere** (the outer solid parts), and the **hydrosphere** (the water parts).
  1. **Meteorology.** The study of weather, climate, and Earth's atmosphere.
  2. **Oceanography.** The study of the oceans and marine organisms.
  3. **Physiography.** The study of the physical features of Earth's surface.
- **Engineering.** The study of applying scientific knowledge for practical purposes.
  1. **Chemical technology engineering.** The branch of engineering concerned with the application of chemistry in the production of goods and services that humankind considers useful.
  2. **Food technology engineering.** The branch of engineering concerned with the application of food science to the selection, preservation, processing, packaging, and distribution of safe, nutritious, and wholesome food.
  3. **Product development engineering.** The branch of engineering concerned with designing, developing, and testing new products.
  4. **Structural engineering.** The branch of engineering concerned with designing

as well as testing the strength of structures, including buildings, bridges, and dams.

- **Mathematics.** The use of numbers and symbols to study amounts and forms.
  1. **Angular apparent measurement.** A measurement in degrees of how far or how large objects appear to be.
  2. **Ratio.** A pair of numbers used to compare quantities.

- **Physics.** The study of forms of energy and the laws of motion.
  1. **Energy.** The capacity to make things change. The process of making them change is called **work**. This is accomplished when a **force (F)** (a push or a pull on an object) causes an object to move, which is the process of transferring energy. Subtopics may include:
     a. **Heat.** The energy transferred between objects because of differences in their temperature.
     b. **Radiant energy.** Energy in the form of waves that can travel through space; also called radiation.
     c. **Sound.** Energy in the form of waves that can only travel through a **medium** (any solid, liquid, or gas).
  2. **Mechanics.** The study of objects in motion and the forces that produce the motion. Subtopics may include:
     a. **Buoyancy.** The upward force of a fluid on an object placed in it, such as water pushing up on a boat.
     b. **Periodic motion.** Any type of motion that successively repeats itself in equal intervals of time.

Chapter 3

Do Topic Research

The third step of the project is research, which is the process of collecting information about a subject. It is also the facts collected. When you do research, you get information from the world around you, from personal experiences, and from knowledgeable sources, including printed works such as magazines and science books, teachers and mentors, and other students. Your first research, called topic research, is used to select a project topic.

How to Select a Topic

Obviously you want to get an A+ on your project, win awards at the science fair, and learn many new things about science. Some or all of these goals are possible, but you will have to spend a lot of time working on your project, so choose a topic that interests you. It is best to pick a topic and stick with it, but if you find after some work that your topic is not as interesting as you originally thought, stop and select another one. Since it takes time to develop a good project, it is unwise to repeatedly jump from one topic to another. You may, in fact, decide to stick with your original idea even if it is not as exciting as you had expected. You might just uncover some very interesting facts that you didn't know.

Remember that the objective of a science project is to learn more about science. Your project doesn't have to be highly complex to be successful. Excellent projects can be developed that answer very basic and fundamental questions about events or situations encountered on a daily basis. There are many easy ways of selecting a topic. The following are just a few of them.

ASK QUESTIONS ABOUT THE WORLD AROUND YOU

You can turn everyday experiences into a project topic by asking **inquiry questions** (questions about a science topic that may or may not be used as the project problem). For example, you may have noticed that a package of paper for your printer has directions that say to place one side up. As both sides of the paper look basically the same, you wonder what the difference might be. If you express this as an inquiry question, you might ask, "Is the ink absorbed better on one side of the paper?" Here you have a good question about physical properties, but could this be a project topic? Think about it!

You can answer this type of question with a simple yes or no, which wouldn't make for a great science project. But what if you kept asking questions? What is the difference between one side of the paper and the other that makes one side absorb the ink better? Is paper with a smooth texture more absorbent than paper with a rough texture? By continuing to ask questions, you zero in on the topic of how the **absorbency** (the ability of a material to hold a liquid) of paper affects the quality of the printing on the paper.

Keep your eyes and ears open, and start asking yourself more inquiry questions. You will be pleasantly surprised at the number of possible project topics that will come to mind when you begin to look around and use inquiry questions.

You and those around you make an amazing number of statements and ask many questions each day that could be used to develop science project topics. Be alert and listen for statements such as, "He gets his red hair from his grandmother." This statement can become an inquiry question: "Why don't children look like their parents?" or "Why do some children look more like their grandparents than their parents?" These questions could lead you to developing a project about heredity.

CHOOSE A TOPIC FROM YOUR EXPERIENCES

You may think that you don't have much experience with science topics, but remember this doesn't have to be rocket science! For example, you know that water in a puddle quickly disappears on a warm day because the heat causes the water to **vaporize** (to change from a liquid to a gas). You observe that ice cubes in a freezer get smaller if left an extended time. Why do the ice cubes get smaller without a change in temperature? Can ice change directly to a gas? These questions can lead you to a project about **sublimation** (the change from a solid to a gas or vice versa).

FIND A TOPIC IN SCIENCE MAGAZINES

Don't expect topic ideas in science magazines to include detailed instructions on how to perform experiments, build models, or design displays. Instead, you can look for facts that interest you and that lead you to ask inquiry questions. An article about minerals found in and near the Grand Canyon in Arizona might bring to mind these inquiry questions: "What is a mineral?" "What makes minerals different from one another?" "How does the solubility of materials in minerals affect their formation?"

SELECT A TOPIC FROM A BOOK ON SCIENCE PROJECTS

Science project books, such as this one, can provide you with many different topics as well as some inquiry questions. If you use a book of science projects, it is still up to you to pick a topic and develop it into your own science fair project. A list of different science project books can be found in the appendix.

PICK A TOPIC BY STUDYING TOPICS OF OTHER SCIENCE FAIR PROJECTS

Part III of this book provides a list of possible science fair project problems. These are organized by category. While you are not encouraged to use these exact problems, you can review them to help you pick your topic.

ISSUES INVOLVING SPECIAL TOPICS

Before beginning your project, discuss your plans with your teacher. He or she will be familiar with the regulations that govern some special topics such as potentially dangerous investigations. These may include the use of certain chemicals and equipment, experimental techniques, or experiments involving live animals, cell cultures, microorganisms, or animal tissues. For some experiments, an adult sponsor trained in the area of your topic will be required to supervise your project. The most important thing is your safety as well as the safety of any other people or animals involved in your project.

If you have not adhered to the rules of the fair, you may not be allowed to enter your completed work. Your project topic should be approved by your teacher before beginning. This prevents you from working on an unsafe project and from wasting time on a project that might be disqualified.

Chapter 4

Do Project Research

By the fourth step, you have completed the topic research and selected a topic, you are ready to begin your project research. This research is generally more thorough than topic research. Project research is an in-depth study of the project topic with the objective of expressing a project purpose, proposing a hypothesis, and designing a project experiment to test the hypothesis. Project research is the process of collecting information from knowledgeable sources, such as books, magazines, and software, or teachers, parents, scientists, or other professionals. It can also include data collected from exploratory experimentation. Read widely on the topic you selected so that you understand it and know about the findings of others. Be sure to give credit where credit is due, and record all information in your journal.

Research Hints

Here are some hints to make research more productive:
1. Use many references from both printed sources—books, journals, magazines, and newspapers—and electronic sources—computer software and online sources.
2. Gather information from professionals—instructors, librarians, and scientists such as researchers, physicians, nurses, and veterinarians.
3. Perform exploratory experiments if applicable for your topic. Many of the projects in Part II can be used as exploratory experiments.

How successful you are with your project will depend largely on how well you understand your topic. The more you read and question people who know something about your topic, the broader your understanding will be. As a result, it will be easier for you to explain your project to other people, especially a science fair judge. There are two basic kinds of research: primary and secondary.

Primary Research

Primary research is information you collect on your own. This includes information from exploratory experiments you perform, surveys you take, interviews you conduct, and responses to your letters.

Interview people who have special knowledge about your topic. You may include teachers, doctors, scientists, or others whose careers require them to know something related to your topic. Let's say your topic is about butterflies. Who would know about **entomology** (the study of insects)? Start with your science teacher. He or she may have a special interest in insects or know someone who does. Is there a museum nearby with an exhibit of butterflies? You could also try the biology department of a local university.

Before contacting the people you want to interview, be prepared. Make a list of questions that you want to ask. Try discussing what you know about your topic with someone who knows nothing about it. This can force you to organize your thinking, and you may even discover additional questions to add to your list. Once your list is complete, you are ready to make your calls.

Simple rules of courtesy will better ensure that the person called is willing to help:
1. Identify yourself.
2. Identify the school you attend and your teacher.
3. Briefly explain why you are calling. Include information about your project and explain how you think the person can help you.
4. Request an interview time that is convenient for the person. This could be a telephone, face-to-face, or e-mail interview. Be sure to say that the interview will take about 20 to 30 minutes.
5. Ask if you may tape-record the interview. You can get more information if you are not trying to write down all the answers. The person may even have time when you call, so be prepared to start the interview.
6. Be on time and be ready to start the interview immediately. Also, be courteous and end the interview on time.
7. If the interview is through e-mail, make sure your questions are understandable and grammatically correct. You might ask someone to edit them before you send them.
8. After the interview, thank the person for his or her time and for the information provided.
9. Even if you send an e-mail thank-you, you may wish to send a written thank-you note as soon as possible after the interview, so be sure to record the person's name and address.

You may write letters requesting information instead of interviewing, or write letters in addition to interviewing. Check at the end of articles in periodicals for lists of names and addresses where you can obtain more information. Your librarian can help you find current periodicals related to your topic. If your project deals with a household product, check the packaging for the address of the manufacturer. Send your letter to the public relations department. Ask for all available printed material about your topic. Sign your letter and send it as soon as possible to allow time for material to be sent back to you. You can use a form letter similar to the one shown here to make it easier to send your questions to as many different people and organizations as you can find.

Lauren Russell
123 Davin Lane
Lacey, TX 00000

June 23, 2006

Wash-Away Corporation
222 Dirt Street
Grime, NY 11111

Dear Director:

I am a sixth-grade student currently working on a science fair project for the David Russell Middle School Science Fair. My project is about the cleaning effect of enzymes in detergent. I would greatly appreciate any information you could send me on the enzymes in your product. Please send the information as soon as possible.

Thank you very much.

Sincerely,

Lauren Russell

Secondary Research

Secondary research is information and/or data that someone else has collected. You may find this type of information in written sources (books, magazines, newspapers, and encyclopedias) and in electronic sources (CD-ROM encyclopedias, software packages, and online). When you use a secondary source, be sure to note where you got the information for future reference. If you are required to write a report, you will need the following information for a bibliography or to give credit for any quotes or illustrations you use:

Book. Author's name, title of book, publisher, city of publication, year of publication, and pages read or quoted.

Magazine or periodical. Author's name, title of article, title of magazine, volume number, issue number, date of publication, and page numbers of article.

Newspaper. Author's name, title of article, name of newspaper, city of publication, date of publication, and section and page numbers.

Encyclopedia. Name of encyclopedia, volume number, title of article, publisher, city of publication, year of publication, and page numbers of article.

CD-ROM encyclopedia or software package. Name of program, version or release number, name of supplier, and place where supplier is located.

Online documents. Author of document (if known), title of document, name of organization that posted the document, place where organization is located, date given on document, and online address or mailing address where document is available.

Chapter 5

Find a Project Problem

The fifth step of your science project is about the need of a definite problem or goal: What do you want to find out? What question do you wish to answer? In summary, what would you like to accomplish? The project problem should identify two variables (the parts of the project that could change). The independent variable is the variable you change. The dependent variable is the variable being observed that changes in response to the independent variable. Your project should have only one independent variable. Therefore, you will know what causes any change you observe in the dependent variable.

The project problem can be a statement or it can be expressed as a question about what you are trying to find out. The problem is the foundation of your whole project, so it's very important to get it right.

A project experiment is a test to determine a relationship between the two variables. A problem for an experimental project must have a measurable dependent variable. For example, in the problem "How do the number of leaves on a plant affect the volume of water lost by transpiration?" the number of leaves is the independent variable, and the volume of water transpired, which can be measured, is the dependent variable. An example of a problem in the form of a statement might be, "To determine the effect of water temperature on the respiration rate of goldfish." In this problem, water temperature is the independent variable, and respiration rate is the dependent variable.

Problem Hints

1. Limit your experimental problem to one independent variable and one dependent variable. Note that in the question "What is the effect of water temperature on the respiration rate of goldfish?" there is one independent variable (water temperature) and one dependent variable (respiration rate). A question such as "How does water temperature affect goldfish?" is not a good problem because there are too many possible dependent variables.

2. Choose an experimental problem that will have measurable results. In the problem "What effect does humidity have on the growth rate of Epsom salt crystals?" the rate of crystal growth can be measured. But the question "How does temperature affect crystals?" gives no clues as to measurable results.

Chapter 6

Come Up with a Project Hypothesis

The sixth step of your project concerns a hypothesis, which is a prediction of the solution to a problem based on knowledge and research. All of your project research is done with the goal of expressing a problem, proposing an answer to it (the hypothesis), and designing a project experiment to test the hypothesis. A hypothesis can be a declarative statement or an "If . . . then . . ." type of statement. Following are examples of hypotheses.

As you learned in chapter 5, the project problem is a question or statement that identifies the independent and dependent variables. For example, "Are moths more attracted to white or yellow light?" The hypothesis should make a claim about how the independent and dependent variables relate. For example, in the sample hypotheses for this problem, the two related variables are light color (independent variable) and attraction of moths to light (dependent variable):

> "Moths will be more attracted to white light than to yellow. This is based on research information that moths use the white light of the Moon to determine direction."

or

> "If the light is similar in color to the Moon, then more moths will be attracted to it. This is based on research information that moths use the white light of the Moon to determine direction."

For the question "Where are the most number of stomata found on leaves?" the location of the stomata is the independent variable, but the dependent variable is not identified. The hypothesis should identify this missing variable. For example, in the sample hypotheses for the problem, the two relating factors are location of the stomata (independent variable) and amount of water lost by transpiration (dependent variable):

> "Exposing only the area of a leaf with the most stomata will cause little to no change in the amount of water lost by transpiration. This is based on the research information that water lost by transpiration is through stomata."

or

> "If the area with the least stomata is covered on a leaf, then there will be little to no change in the amount of water lost by transpiration. This is based on the research information that water lost by transpiration is through stomata."

Hypothesis Hints

1. State facts from research, including past experiences or observations on which you based your research hypothesis.
2. Write down your hypothesis before beginning the project experimentation.
3. Don't change your hypothesis even if experimentation does not support it. If time permits, repeat the experiment to confirm your results.

Chapter 7

Design a Project Experiment

By this seventh step, you should have decided on a specific type of project, its problem, and your hypothesis. Now you are ready to design an experiment to test your hypothesis. Following are examples for designing a project experiment.

Can you think of a way to test your hypothesis experimentally with measurable results? If the answer is no, then you need to go back to the previous step and reword your hypothesis or select another one.

A project experiment is designed to test a hypothesis. It is a test that determines a relationship between an independent variable and a dependent variable. For example, for the project problem "Which color light, white or yellow, are moths most attracted to?" the hypothesis is "If the light is similar in color to the Moon, then more moths will be attracted to it. This is based on research information that moths use the light of the Moon to determine direction." The independent variable for the experiment is light color and the dependent variable is the attraction of the moth to one color or another. The variables that should be kept constant are controlled variables. The controlled variables include the type of lightbulb used, including size, wattage, and incandescence, total time of observation, method of counting moths, time of year, time of day, atmospheric conditions, and so on. It's important to think of all the possible variables when setting up your experiment to be sure they won't change.

A possible experiment to determine which color of light moths are most attracted to involves using white and yellow 75-watt incandescent lightbulbs. Test one color lightbulb at a time outdoors using a desk lamp and a white poster board screen. Count the number of moths on or within 6 inches (15 cm) from the screen during a 2-minute period, first after each light has been on for 30 minutes and again after the light has been off for 30 minutes. The procedure should be repeated four or more times on different nights.

A control is a standard for comparison. The control is identical with the project experiment except for the independent variable. In the moth project, the independent variable is the color of light; thus, the control could be the absence of light to determine if in fact it is light that attracts moths. The experiment should be repeated without any light.

Note that in some experiments a control is not a separate experimental setup. Instead, it can be the independent variable selected as the basis for comparison. For example, if the problem is "How does white, red, blue, and yellow light affect the attraction of moths?" the experiment would be to determine the attraction of moths to the different light colors. The white light, being the most common color of light, could arbitrarily be selected as the control and the results of the other lights compared to it.

Experimentation Hints

When designing your project experiment, remember:

1. Include a way of measuring the results. For example, to measure the number of moths, you need to choose a specific area where the moths will be counted (on or within 6 inches [15 cm] from the screen) as well as the period of time for counting (2 minutes).
2. Be sure to have only one independent variable during the experiment.
3. Repeat the experiment more than once to verify your results. For the sample moth experiment, the test is repeated in exactly the same way on four or more different nights. While some of the controlled variables, such as those relating to weather, may vary from night to night, this would not affect the results because the controlled variables would be the same on any specific night for the testing of each colored light on that night.
4. Have a control and repeat the control along with the rest of the experiment.
5. Carefully record and organize the data from your experiment. (See Step 8 for information on organizing data from an experiment.)
6. Have an adult supervise you if necessary for safety. (The teacher who approves your project should tell you if adult supervision is needed.)
7. Use necessary safety equipment, such as safety goggles, and procedures, such as not substituting materials or using unfamiliar tools. (Check with your project adviser about these issues.)

Now that you have a basic design for your experiment, you are ready to put together a step-by-step testing procedure that includes the materials and time you will need. For some experiments in which time is a factor, such as one measuring the growth of plants over time, four or more identical sets of plants as well as the control could be started at the same time. Be prepared to record all the results in your project log book. All results should include the date and the time if applicable.

Experimental data from your project and what you do with it is the main evaluation criterion. Judges like to see charts (data or other information in the form of tables, graphs, or lists) of the measured results. If judges can clearly see the results of a project, they are likely to give the project a higher score. If there is no data displayed, then judges are likely to conclude that the student doesn't understand how to properly develop a science fair project. (For more information about data, see chapter 8.)

Chapter 8

Collect Raw Data

This eighth step describes types of and ways to collect raw data (experimental results). **Raw data** includes **observations** (information collected about something by using your senses) made during testing. The two types of observations are qualitative and quantitative. A **quantitative observation** is a description of the amount of something. Numbers are used in quantitative descriptions. Instruments, such as a balance, a ruler, and a timer, are used to measure quantities or to describe the amount of the property being observed, such as mass, height, or time.

Metric measurements are generally the preferred units of measurement for science fair projects; for example, length in meters, mass in grams, volume in milliliters, and temperature in degrees Celsius. Another type of quantitative observation can be a scale that you design. For example, if your experiment involves measuring the change in the freshness of flowers, you might have a scale of freshness from 1 to 5, with 5 being the most fresh and having no dry parts on the petals and 1 being the least fresh with each petal being totally dry.

A **qualitative observation** is a description of the physical properties of something, including how it looks, sounds, feels, smells, and/or tastes. Words are used in a qualitative description. The qualitative description of a light could be about its color and would include words such as white, yellow, blue, and red.

As you collect raw data, record it in your log book. You want your log to be organized and neat, but you should not recopy the raw data for your journal. You should recopy the data that you will want to represent the information on your display in tables and/or graphs so that it is more easily understandable and meaningful to observers. (See chapter 10 for information about the project display.)

Tables

Data is generally recorded in a **table**, which is a chart in which information is arranged in rows and columns. A **column** is a vertical listing of data values and a **row** is a horizontal listing of data values. There are different ways of designing a table, but all tables should have a **title** (a descriptive heading) and rows and columns that are labeled. If your table shows measurements, the units of measurement, such as minutes or centimeters, should be part of the column's or row's label.

For an experimental data table, such as Table 8.1, the title generally describes the dependent variable of the experiment, such as "Moths' Attraction to Light," which in this case is for the data from an experiment where yellow and white lightbulbs (independent variable) are used and the number of moths attracted to each light is counted (dependent variable). In contrast, the title "White Light versus Yellow Light in the Attraction of Moths" expresses what is being compared. As a key part of the data organization, an average of each of the testings is calculated.

Table 8.1. Moths' Attraction to Light

Light Color	Test 1	Test 2	Test 3	Test 4	Average
White	11	13	11	13	12
Yellow	4	3	5	4	4
Control (no light)	2	0	0	2	1

Analyzing and Interpreting Data

When you have finished collecting the data from your project, the next step is to interpret and analyze it. To **analyze** means to examine, compare, and relate all the data. To **interpret** the data means to restate it, which involves reorganizing it into a more easily understood form, such as by graphing it. A **graph** is a visual representation of data that shows a relationship between two variables. All graphs should have:

1. A title.
2. Titles for the *x*-axis (horizontal) and *y*-axis (vertical).
3. Scales with numbers that have the same interval between each division.
4. Labels for the categories being counted. Scales often start at zero, but they don't have to.

The three most common graphs used in science fair projects are the bar graph, the circle graph, and the line graph. Graphs are easily prepared using graphing software on a computer. But if these tools are not available to you, here are hints for drawing each type of graph.

In a **bar graph**, you use solid bar-like shapes to show the relationship between the two variables. Bar graphs can have vertical or horizontal bars. The width and separation of each bar should be the same. The length of a bar represents a specific number on a scale, such as 10 moths. The width of a bar is not significant and can depend on available space due to the number of bars needed. A bar graph has one scale, which can be on the horizontal or vertical axis. This type of graph is most often used when the independent variable is qualitative, such as the number of moths in Table 8.1. The independent variable for the Moths' Attraction to Light table is the color of light—white, yellow, or no light (control)—and the dependent variable for this data is the number of moths near each light. A bar graph using the data from Table 8.1 is shown in Figure 8.1. Since the average number of moths from the data varies from 1 to 12, a scale of 0 to 15 was used, with each unit of the scale representing 1 moth. The heights of the bars in the bar graph show clearly that some moths were found in the area without light and some near the yellow light, but the greatest number were present in the area with white light.

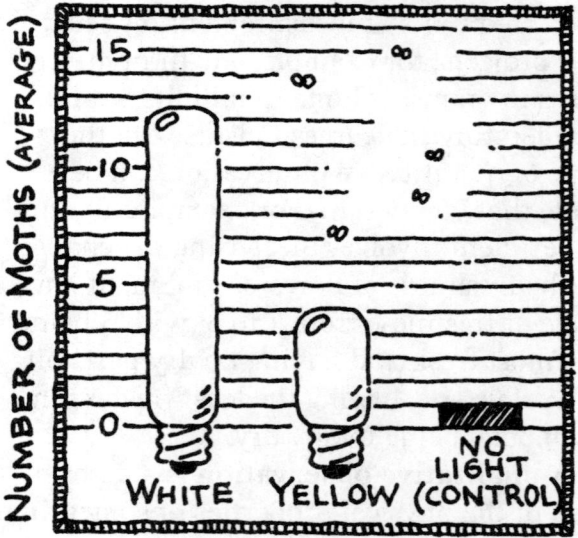

Figure 8.1. Example of a bar graph.

A **circle graph** (also called a **pie chart**) is a graph in which the area of a circle represents a sum of data, and the sizes of the pie-shaped pieces into which the circle is divided represent the amount of data. To plot your data on a circle graph, you need to calculate the size of each section. An entire circle represents 360°, so each section of a circle graph is a fraction of 360°. For example, data from Table 8.1 was used to prepare the circle graph in Figure 8.2. The size of each section in degrees was determined using the following steps:

1. Express the ratio of each section as a fraction, with the numerator equal to the average number of moths counted on each type of light and the denominator equal to the average total number of moths counted on all the lights:

    White = $12/17$

    Yellow = $4/17$

    Control = $1/17$

2. Multiply the fraction by 360°:

    White $12/17 \times 360° = 254.1°$

    Yellow $4/17 \times 360° = 84.7°$

    Control $1/17 \times 360° = 21.2°$

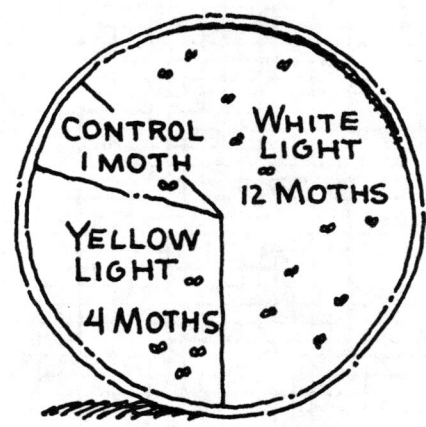

Figure 8.2. Example of a circle graph.

To prepare the circle graph, first decide on the diameter needed, then use a compass to draw a circle. Next draw a straight line from the center of the circle to any point on the edge of the circle. Using a protractor, start at this line and mark a dot on the edge of the circle 254.1° from the line. Draw a line to connect this dot to the center of the circle. The pie-shaped section you made represents the number of moths found near the white light. Start the next section on the outside line for the yellow light section. The remaining section will be the no-light section, or control section. Each section should be labeled as shown in Figure 8.2.

Each section of a circle graph represents part of the whole, which always equals 100%. The larger the section, the greater the percentage of the whole. So all of the sections added together must equal 100%.

To determine the percentage of each section, follow these steps:

1. Change the fractional ratio for each section to a decimal by dividing the numerator by the denominator:

    White light: $12/17 = .70$

    Yellow light: $4/17 = .24$

    Control: $1/17 = .06$

2. Change the decimal answers to percent. *Percent* means "per hundred." For example, for white light, .70 is read $70/100$ or 70 per 100, which can be written as 70%.

    White light: $.70 = 70/100 = 70\%$

    Yellow light: $.24 = 24/100 = 24\%$

    Control: $.06 = 6/100 = 6\%$

To represent the percentage of moths attracted to each light color, you could color each section of the circle graph with a different color. You could label the percentages on the graph and make a legend explaining the colors of each section as in Figure 8.3.

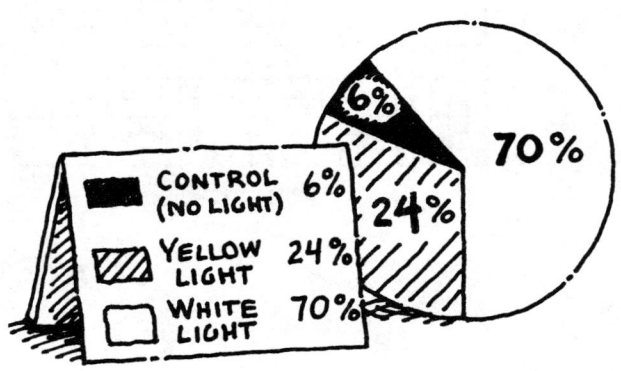

Figure 8.3. Example of a circle graph and a legend.

A **line graph** is a graph in which one or more lines are used to show the relationship between the two quantitative variables. The line shows a pattern of change. While a bar graph has one scale, a line graph has two scales. Figure 8.4 shows a line graph of data from a different study in which the problem was to determine if ants communicate by laying a scent trail for other ants to follow to a food source. The line graph shows data for the number of ants observed on one of the paths every 15 minutes for 1 hour. Generally, the independent variable is on the ***x*-axis** (the vertical axis) and the dependent variable is on the ***y*-axis** (the horizontal axis). For this example, the independent variable of time is on the *x*-axis and the dependent variable of number of ants is on the *y*-axis. One unit on the time scale represents 1 minute, and units are marked off in groups of 15 up to a total of 60 units. One unit on the number of ants scale represents 1 ant. Since the largest average counted was 32.2 ants, the scale for ants is numbered by fives from 0 to 35. On the graph, the increase in the angle of the line over time shows that more ants were found on the food as time increased.

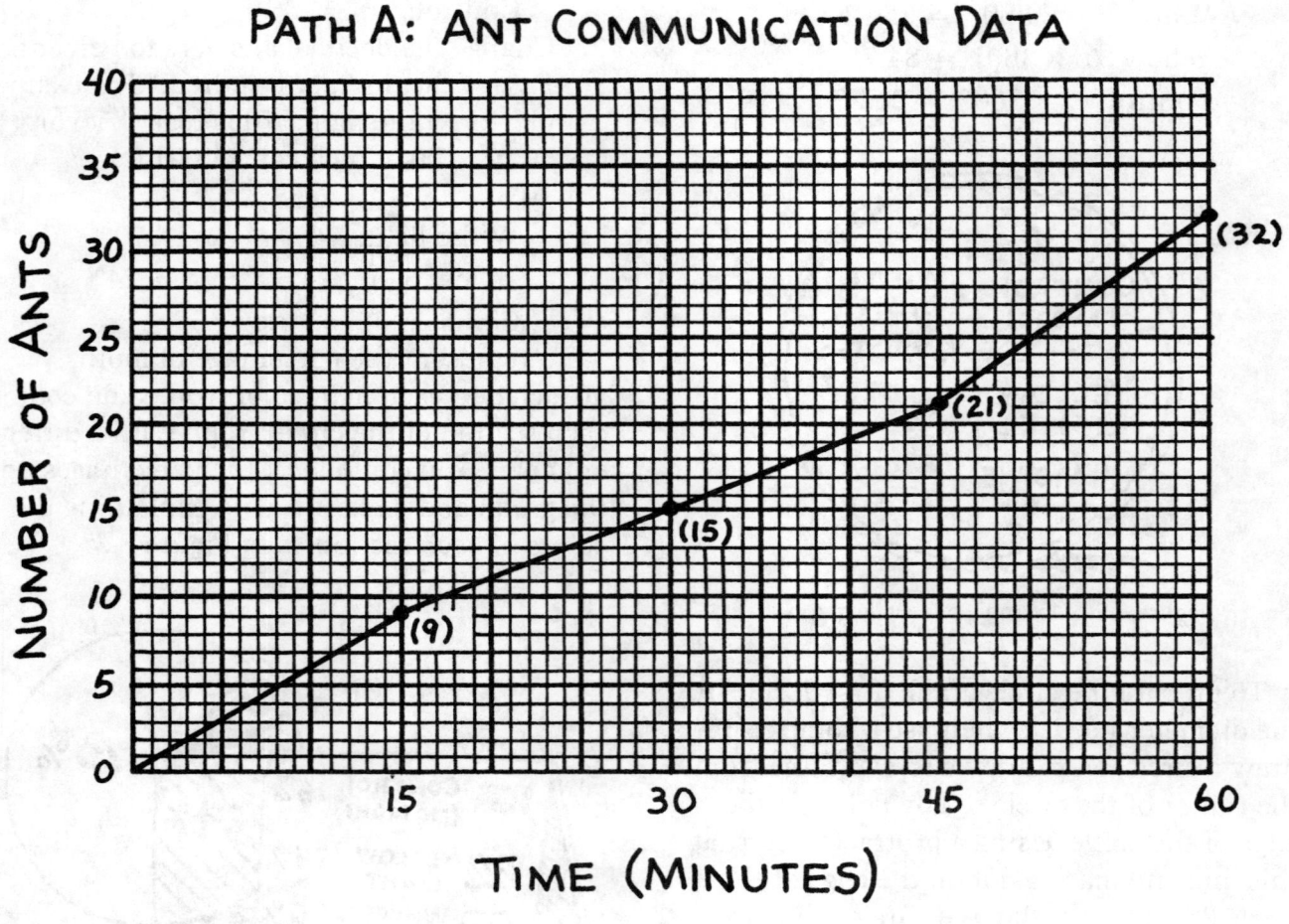

Figure 8.4. Example of a line graph.

Chapter 9

Create Your Project Summaries

By this ninth step, you are ready to prepare your project summaries. Most science fairs require that projects include project summaries. The project summaries include an abstract and a research paper. This chapter gives information and examples for a project abstract and a research paper. Before writing your project summaries, decide on a **project title** (a descriptive heading of the project), which will appear on your abstract, on the title page of your research paper, and prominently on your display backboard. The project title should capture the theme of the project and be intriguing. Its purpose is to attract the attention of observers and make them want to know more. There are no set rules for the length of the title, but it should be short enough to be read at a glance. A rule of thumb is that it should be about 10 words or less. A good title for the sample project about moths' attraction to colored lights is "White or Yellow? Attraction of Moths to Light." Also check with your teacher about the requirements for the science fair you are entering.

Project Abstract

An abstract is a brief overview of the project. It should be no more than one page long and a maximum of 250 words. It includes the title "Abstract," a project title, a statement of purpose, a hypothesis, a brief summary of your experiment procedure, data, and conclusions. The abstract is generally required to be part of the display. (For information about designing your project display, see chapter 10.) This gives judges something to refer to when making final decisions. The abstract is a very important representation of your project, so be sure to do a thorough job on this part of your report.

No school or student name should appear in the abstract.

ABSTRACT

White or Yellow? Attraction of Moths to Light

The purpose of this project is to determine if moths are more attracted to white light than to yellow light. The hypothesis was that since moths use the white light of the Moon to determine direction, they will be more attracted to white light because they mistake it for moonlight. The project experiment involved recording the number of moths near a white light and a yellow light. This was done by testing each light separately. After each light was on for 30 minutes, moths near the lights were counted during a 2-minute observation period. The control had no light. The number of moths near the lights and without light were compared.

The number of moths near the white light was much greater than the number near the yellow light or the area without light. This result confirmed that moths are more attracted to white light than to yellow light.

Figure 9.1. Example of an abstract.

Project Report

Your project report is a written report of your entire project from start to finish. The project report should be clear and detailed enough for a reader who is unfamiliar with your project to know exactly what you did, why you did it, what the results were, whether the experimental evidence supported your hypothesis, and where you got your research information. This written document is your spokesperson when you are not present to explain your project, but more than that, it documents all your work.

Because you'll be recording everything in your project log book as the project progresses, all you need to do in preparing the project report is to organize and neatly copy the desired material from the book's contents. Check with your teacher for the order and content of the report as regulated by the fair in which you are entering the project. Most science fairs require that the report be typewritten, double spaced, and bound in a folder or notebook. It should contain a title page, a table of contents, an introduction, an experiment, discussion, a conclusion, acknowledgments, and references. The rest of this chapter describes these parts of a project report and gives examples based on the sample moth project.

TITLE PAGE

This is the first page of the report. The project title should be centered on the page, and your name, school, and grade should appear in the lower right-hand corner.

TABLE OF CONTENTS

This is the second page of your report. The table of contents should contain a list of everything in the report that follows this page, including a page number for the beginning of each section, as shown in Figure 9.2.

CONTENTS

1. Introduction 1
2. Experiment 2
3. Discussion 3
4. Conclusion 11
5. Acknowledgments......................12
6. References 13

Figure 9.2. Example of a table of contents.

INTRODUCTION

This section sets the stage for your project report. It is a statement of your purpose, along with some of the background information that led you to make this study and what you hoped to achieve from it. It should

INTRODUCTION

Moths are seen flying around outdoor lights at night. Before starting the project, my research uncovered the idea that moths navigate by moonlight. Thus, a moth trying to fly in a straight line could do so by always keeping the Moon to the same side. This method of navigation would fail for artificial lights, possibly causing the moths to endlessly circle the light source.

After observing that some outdoor lights are yellow, I was inspired to create a project to determine if moths are more attracted to white light or to yellow light. Based on previously stated research, my hypothesis was that moths would be more attracted to white light; therefore, there should be more moths flying near a white outdoor light than near a yellow outdoor light.

Figure 9.3. Example of an introduction.

contain a brief statement of your hypothesis based on your research; that is, it should state what information or knowledge led you to your hypothesis. If your teacher requires footnotes, then include one for each information source you have used. The sample introduction shown in Figure 9.3 does not use footnotes.

EXPERIMENT

This part of the report contains information about the project experiment. Describe in detail all methods used to collect your data or make your observations. It should include the project problem followed by a list of the materials used and the amount of each, then the procedural steps in outline or

EXPERIMENT

Problem
Which color light, white or yellow, are moths most attracted to?

Materials
masking tape
20-by-20-inch (50-by-50-cm) piece of white poster board
box with one side at least 20 by 20 inches (50 by 50 cm)
desk lamp
two 75-watt lightbulbs: one white, one yellow
outdoor electrical extension cord if necessary to plug in the lamp (Note: For safety, use an extension cord designed for outdoor use.)
timer

Procedure
1. Prepare a screen by taping the poster board to the side of the box.
2. For 4 nights, place the box on an outside table so that the white poster board screen is 4 feet (1.2 m) from one end of the table.
3. With the desk lamp disconnected from any electrical supply, screw in the white lightbulb.
4. Set the lamp on the table and turn its bulb so that it is 2 feet from and centered on the white poster board screen.
5. After dark, plug in the lamp and turn the light on.
6. After 30 minutes, stand at the end of the table facing the white screen. The lamp will be between you and the screen. Set the timer for 2 minutes and start counting the number of moths that can be seen on or near the screen. Record the number of moths in a table.
7. At the end of 2 minutes, turn the light off.
8. After 30 minutes of darkness, replace the white bulb with the yellow bulb.
9. Repeat steps 5, 6, and 7.
10. After 30 minutes of darkness, turn the light on for 2 minutes and count the moths on or near the screen. Note: The control is when you use no light.
11. Compare the number of moths that you saw on the screens with different-colored lights.

Figure 9.4. Example of an experiment.

paragraph form as shown in Figure 9.4. The experiment described in Figure 9.4 includes instructions for counting the moths. Other things you should include, if they apply, are photographs and instructions for making self-designed equipment. All instructions should be written so that they could be followed by anyone to get the same results.

DISCUSSION

The discussion of your experimental results is a principal part of your project report. It describes the outcome of your efforts. Include experimental data tables and graphs to confirm results. (See Step 8 for information on collecting and organizing your data.) Include qualitative as well as quantitative results. Never change or omit results because they don't support your hypothesis. Be thorough. You want your readers to see your train of thought so that they know exactly what you did. Compare your results with published data and commonly held beliefs, as well as with your expected results. Include a discussion of possible errors. Were your results affected by uncontrolled events? What would you do differently if you repeated this project?

PROJECT CONCLUSION

The **project conclusion** is a summary of the results of the project experiment and a statement of how the results relate to the hypothesis. In one page or less, it tells what you discovered based on your analysis of the data. A sample conclusion is shown in Figure 9.5. The conclusion states the hypothesis and indicates whether the data supports it.

If your results are not what you expected, don't panic. Assuming that your research led you to your hypothesis, state that while your research backed up your hypothesis,

CONCLUSION

As stated in my hypothesis, moths are more attracted to white light than to yellow light. The experimental observation over a period of 1½ hours each night for 4 days showed that more moths fly around a white light than a yellow light. This data supported my hypothesis and indicated that using a yellow lightbulb as an outdoor light will limit the number of moths found in an area where a light is on.

Figure 9.5. Example of a project report conclusion.

your experimental results did not. Refer to any published data on which you based your hypothesis. Say what you expected and what actually happened. Give reasons why you think the results did not support your original ideas. Include errors you might have made as well as how uncontrolled variables might have affected the results. Discuss changes you would make to the procedure if you repeated the project, and include ideas for experiments to further investigate the topic of your project. All information in the conclusion should have been reported in other parts of the report; no new material should be introduced in the conclusion.

ACKNOWLEDGMENTS

The acknowledgments section is a short paragraph or two stating the names of people who helped you, with a brief description of their contributions to your project, as shown in Figure 9.6. It should not be just a list of names. Note that when acknowledging relatives, it is generally not necessary to include their names, just their relationship to you; for example, mother, father, sister,

> **ACKNOWLEDGMENTS**
>
> I would like to thank the members of my family who assisted me with this project: my mother, who copy edited my report, and my father and sister, who assisted in the construction of the display board.
>
> A special note of thanks to Dr. Taylor Bolden, professor of entomology at MaKenzie University, and to Christopher Eugene, his assistant, for their expert guidance.

Figure 9.6. Example of the acknowledgments section of a project report.

and so on. Identify individuals with their titles, positions, and affiliations (institutions), and list anyone who gave financial support or material donations. Do not include the monetary amounts of donations.

REFERENCES

Your reference list is a bibliography of all the sources where you obtained information. See the section "Secondary Research" in chapter 4.

Chapter 10

Design Your Project Display

The tenth step of your **project display** is a visual representation of all the work that you have done. It should consist of a backboard and anything else that supports your project, such as models, exhibits or examples, photographs, surveys, and the like. It must tell the story of the project in such a way that it attracts and holds the interest of the viewers. It has to be thorough but not too crowded, so keep it simple, well organized, attractive, and, most of all, informative. Your teacher can advise you about materials that cannot be displayed as well as those that are required, such as your abstract.

The size and shape allowed for the display backboard can vary, so you will have to check the rules for your science fair. Most displays are allowed to be as large as 48 inches (122 cm) wide, 30 inches (76 cm) deep, and 108 inches (274 cm) high (including the table on which the display is placed). Of course, your display may be smaller, but most participants prefer to take advantage of all the possible space. A three-sided backboard is usually the best way to display your work. Some office supply stores and most scientific supply companies sell inexpensive premade backboards. (Ask your teacher for information about science supply companies.) You can purchase the backboard or build your own. Just remember to use materials that are not likely to be damaged during transportation to the fair. Sturdy cardboard or wooden panels can be cut and hinged together.

Purchased backboards generally come in two colors: black and white. You can make them different colors by covering the backboard with self-stick colored shelving paper or cloth. For items placed on the backboard, select colors that stand out but don't distract the viewer from the material being presented. For example, if the background material is fluorescent, the bright color will be what catches the eye instead of your work.

The title and other headings should be neat and large enough to be read at a distance of about 3 feet (1 m). A short title is often eye-catching. For the title and headings, self-stick letters of various sizes and colors can be purchased at office supply stores and stuck to the backboard. You can cut your own letters out of construction paper or stencil letters directly onto the backboard. You can also use a computer to print the title and other headings.

Some teachers have rules about the position of the information on the backboard. If your teacher doesn't, just put the project title at the top of the center panel and organize the remaining material in some logical order neatly on the rest of the board. Typical headings are "Problem," "Hypothesis," "Procedure" (materials and step-by-step instructions for your project experiment, model, or collection), "Data" (tables and graphs), "Results" (short summary of data), "Conclusion," and "Next Time." Figure 10.1 shows one way of placing the material. The heading "Next Time," though not always required, would follow the conclusion and contain a brief description of plans for future development of the project. Alternately, this infor-

Figure 10.1. Example of a project display.

mation could be included in the conclusion rather than under a separate heading.

Typed material can be placed on a colored backing, such as construction paper. Leave a border of about ¼ to ½ inch (0.63 to 1.25 cm) around the edges of each piece of typed material. Use a paper cutter so that the paper edges will be straight.

You want a display that the judges will remember positively. Before you glue everything down, lay the board on a flat surface and arrange the materials a few different ways. This will help you decide on the most suitable and attractive presentation.

Helpful Hints

1. Make sure the display represents the current year's work only.
2. The title should attract the interest of a casual observer. Not only should the title itself be interesting, but it should stand out visually.
3. Organization is a very important part of designing a display. You want a logical order so that observers (especially judges) can easily follow the development of your project from start to finish. Before you actually stick anything to the board, make a diagram of where each part will be placed.
4. One way to arrange the letters on the backboard is to first lay the letters out on the board without attaching them. Then use a yardstick (meter stick) and pencil to draw a straight, light guideline where the bottom of each letter should line up. This will help you keep the lettering straight. Before sticking everything down, you may wish to seek the opinion of other students, teachers, or family members.
5. If you need electricity for your project, be sure the wiring meets all safety standards.
6. Bring an emergency kit to the science fair that includes anything you think you might need to make last-minute repairs to the display, such as extra letters, glue, tape, construction paper that is the same color as the backboard, a stapler, scissors, pencils, pens, touch-up paint, markers, and so forth.
7. If allowed, before standing your backboard on the display table, cover the table with a colored cloth. Choose a color that matches the color scheme of the backboard. This will help to separate your project from other projects displayed on either side.

Do's and Don'ts

Do adhere to the size limitations and safety rules set by the fair. Generally, the size limitations are 48 inches (122 cm) wide, 30 inches (76 cm) deep, and 108 inches (274 cm) high (including the table on which the display is placed).

Do use computer-generated graphs or ones that are very neatly prepared.

Do display photos representing the procedure and the results.

Do use contrasting colors.

Do limit the number of colors used.

Do display models when applicable for experiment projects. If possible, make the models match the color scheme of the backboard.

Do attach charts neatly. If there are many, place them on top of each other so that the top chart can be lifted to reveal the ones below.

Do balance the arrangement of materials on the backboard; that is, evenly distribute the materials on the board so that they cover about the same amount of space on each panel.

Do use rubber cement or double-sided tape to attach papers. White school glue causes the paper to wrinkle.

Do have one or more people review all of your work before you put it on the backboard.

Don't leave large empty spaces on the backboard.

Don't leave the table in front of the backboard empty. Display your models (if any), report, copies of your abstract, and your data book here.

Don't hang electrical equipment on the backboard so that the electric cord runs down the front of the backboard.

Don't make the title or headings hard to read by using uneven lettering or words with letters of different colors.

Don't hand-print the letters on the backboard.

Don't attach folders that fall open on the backboard.

Don't make spelling mistakes, mathematical errors, or errors in writing chemical formulas.

Safety

Anything that is or could be hazardous to other students or the public is prohibited and cannot be displayed. Your teacher has access to a complete list of safety rules from your local science fair officials. Models or photographs can be used instead of things that are restricted from display. The following items are generally unacceptable for display:

- Live animals
- Microbial cultures or fungi, living or dead
- Animal or human parts, except for teeth, hair, nails, and dried animal bones
- Liquids, including water
- Chemicals and/or their empty containers, including caustics, acids, and household cleaners
- Open or concealed flames
- Batteries with open-top cells
- Combustible materials
- Aerosol cans of household solvents
- Controlled substances, poisons, or drugs
- Any equipment or device that would be hazardous to the public
- Sharp items, such as syringes, knives, and needles
- Gases

Chapter 11

Prepare an Oral Presentation and Plan for Your Evaluation

This eleventh step provides clues for preparing for presentations and judging of your project. Your teacher may require that you give an oral presentation on your project for your class. Make it short but complete. Presenting in front of your classmates may be the hardest part of the project. You want to do your best, so prepare and practice, practice, practice. If possible, tape your practice presentation on a tape recorder or have someone videotape you. Review the tape or video and evaluate yourself. Review your notes and practice again.

Practicing an oral presentation will also be helpful for the science fair itself. The judges give points for how clearly you are able to discuss the project and explain its purpose, procedure, results, and conclusion. Judges are impressed with students who can speak confidently about their work. They are not interested in memorized speeches—they will want to have a conversation with you to determine if you understand the work you have done from start to finish. While the display should be organized so that it explains everything, your ability to discuss your project and answer questions convinces the judges that you did the work and understand what you have done. Practice a speech in front of friends and invite them to ask questions. If you do not know the answer to a question, never guess or make up an answer or say you don't know something. Instead, say that you did not discover that answer during your research, then offer other information that you found of interest about the project. Be proud of the project, and approach the judges with enthusiasm about your work.

As you progress through your project, keep in mind that you may be asked about different developmental stages. Take note of some of the ideas that you had while working on your project. These can be used to hold an audience's interest and impress judges.

You can decide on how best to dress for a class presentation. It is wise to make a special effort to look nice for the local fair. You are representing your work. In effect, you are acting as a salesperson for your project, and you want to present the very best image possible. Your appearance shows how much pride you have in yourself, and that is the first step in introducing your product, your science project.

About Judging

Most fairs have similar point systems for judging projects. You may be better prepared if you understand that a judge generally starts by assuming that each student's project is average. Then he or she adds or subtracts points from that average mark. A student should receive points for accomplishing the following, or have points deducted if any of these tasks have not been accomplished:

1. Project Objectives
   - Presenting original ideas
   - Stating the problem clearly
   - Defining the variables and using controls

- Relating background reading to the problem

2. Project Skills
   - Being knowledgeable about equipment used
   - Performing the experiments with little or no assistance except as required for safety
   - Demonstrating the skills required to do all the work necessary to obtain the reported data

3. Data Collection
   - Using a journal to collect data and research
   - Repeating the experiment to verify the results
   - Spending an appropriate amount of time to complete the project
   - Having measurable results

4. Data Interpretation
   - Using tables, graphs, and illustrations in interpreting data
   - Using research to interpret collected data
   - Collecting enough data to reach a conclusion
   - Using only collected data to make a conclusion

5. Project Presentation (Written Materials/Interview/Display)
   - Having a complete and comprehensive report
   - Answering questions accurately
   - Using the display during an oral presentation
   - Justifying conclusions on the basis of experimental data
   - Summarizing what was learned
   - Presenting a display that shows creative ability and originality
   - Presenting an attractive and interesting display

Do's and Don'ts at the Fair

Do bring activities, such as puzzles to work on or a book to read, to keep yourself occupied at your booth. There may be a lengthy wait before the first judge arrives and even between judges.

Do become acquainted with your neighboring presenters. Be friendly and courteous.

Do ask neighboring presenters about their projects and tell them about yours if they express interest. These conversations pass time and help relieve nervous tension that can build when you are waiting to be evaluated. You may also discover research techniques that you can use for next year's project.

Do have fun!

Don't laugh or talk loudly with your neighbor.

Don't forget that you are an ambassador for your school. Your attitude and behavior influence how people at the fair think about you and the other students at your school.

Part II

40 Sample Projects

Project 1

What Effect Does the Physical Form of a Fertilizer Have on Plant Growth?

Category: **Agriculture—Fertilizer**
Project Idea by: **Valerie Kaman**

A **fertilizer** is a soil additive containing plant **nutrients** (nourishing materials necessary for life and growth). There are 16 elements known to be necessary for a plant's growth and survival. **Elements** are basic chemical substances. Soil is often lacking in nitrogen (N), phosphorus (P), and potassium (K). These elements are called **primary nutrients** and are included in most fertilizers. A **complete fertilizer** refers to any mixture containing all three primary nutrients. This type of fertilizer is described by a set of three numbers. For example, 5–8–7 designates a fertilizer containing 5 percent nitrogen, 8 percent phosphorus, and 7 percent potassium.

The **secondary nutrients** are calcium (Ca), magnesium (Mg), and sulfur (S). Soils usually contain enough of these nutrients, but if not, they can be added.

Elements that are necessary for plant growth but are needed in only very small amounts are sometimes called **trace elements**. These elements are boron (B), copper (Cu), iron (Fe), chloride (Cl), manganese (Mn), molybdenum (Mo), and zinc (Zn). Decomposing (breaking down into simpler parts) materials such as grass clippings and tree leaves are good sources of trace elements for plants. Hydrogen (H), oxygen (O), and carbon (C) are necessary elements that generally come from air and water.

Vascular plants, including trees, bushes, and most flowers, contain tubelike structures that transport nutrients. Water and other nutrients in the soil are taken in by the plant roots and transported through a tubelike structure called the **xylem**. Fertilizers come in different physical forms including solid sticks, powder, liquid, and even gas. Does the form of a fertilizer affect its ability to be taken in by the roots and transported through the xylem of plants? A project question might be, "What effect does the physical form of a fertilizer have on plant growth?"

Clues for Your Investigation

Grow plants from seeds, such as pinto beans, in pots. Plant 10 seeds in each of four different pots. One pot will receive no fertilizer, and the remaining three pots will each receive a different physical form of plant fertilizer: liquid, dry-powdered, or dry-stick. Label each pot with the type of fertilizer it receives. The pot getting no fertilizer should be labeled "control." To ensure that the different forms of fertilizer have the same chemical composition, use dry sticks to prepare the other forms. Crush the sticks to make powdered fertilizer. For liquid fertilizer, crush the sticks and add just enough water to dissolve all the fertilizer. Each plant should receive the same amount of fertilizer regardless of the form and be watered with an equal amount of water. Observe the pots periodically for a certain amount of time. Determine a way to measure the growth of the plants such as measuring the length of the stems. The growth of the plants should be recorded and compared to determine which type of fertilizer results in the fastest growth rate.

Independent Variable: Different physical forms of plant food—liquid, powdered, stick

Dependent Variable: Growth rate of plants

Controlled Variables: Amount and composition of fertilizer; environmental conditions including temperature, light, and humidity; and amount of water given to each plant

Control: Plants without added fertilizer

Other Questions to Explore

1. What effect does the planting medium have on plant growth?
2. What effect does the texture of soil have on plant growth?
3. What effect does the deficiency of certain minerals have on plant growth?

Project 2

What Effect Does Talcum Powder Have as an Insecticide?

Category: **Agriculture—Insect Pest Management**
Project Idea by: **Thomas Shulanberger**

A **pesticide** is a substance intended to repel, kill, or control any kind of **pest** (an unwanted organism). Pests include weeds and insects. Pesticides used to kill weeds and insects are called **herbicides** and **insecticides**, respectively.

In an effort to kill mosquitoes, the chemical insecticide dichloro-diphenyl-trichloroethane, commonly called DDT, used to be sprayed from planes. It was very effective in killing insects. The problem was that it was not selective and killed good as well as bad insects. It also caused many problems in animals including the loss of calcium from the shells of bird eggs. This loss caused the eggs to be soft and easily cracked, preventing baby birds from developing. In 1972, DDT was **banned** (forbidden to be used) in the United States. Many other nations have banned it or put it under strict control.

Because of the negative effects of some pesticides, organic pesticides are used by some gardeners and farmers. **Organic pesticides** are pesticides that come from natural sources, including plants such as marigolds, and minerals such as boric acid.

Boric acid is an effective organic insecticide that kills insects that eat it. Sugar is often mixed with borax to attract insects. Talcum powder is said to be an effective organic insecticide that repels ants. Some report that ants will not walk through the powder. How much powder is needed to stop the ants? Is it the depth of the powder or the width of the trail that makes the powder an effective ant insecticide? Does talcum powder repel other insects? A project question might be, "What effect does talcum powder have as an insecticide?"

Clues for Your Investigation

Design a method for testing the effectiveness of talcum powder as an insecticide. One way is to catch and count insects in areas surrounded by various amounts of talcum powder as well as an area with no powder. Since some insects are harmful, including some ants, the collecting method must be safe, such as an insect-collecting trap. You can prepare a trap by digging a hole in the ground large enough to hold a plastic jar. The top of the jar should be just barely above ground. Place a ring of talcum powder around the open mouth of the jar. For each testing site, vary the width of the powder ring but keep the depth the same. The control will have no powder. After a predetermined time, secure labeled lids on each jar that identify the width of the powder ring. Then lift the jars out of the ground and count the insects inside. The testing sites should all be in the same general area. Release the captured insects in the area they were caught

Independent Variable: Width of the talcum powder ring around an insect trap

Dependent Variable: Number of trapped insects

Controlled Variables: Type of powder, concentration of powder in the rings, type of collecting jar, and environmental conditions

Control: Collecting jar without powder

Other Questions to Explore

1. Foods, including onions, garlic, and cayenne (red) pepper, are said to be insecticides. Do these insecticides kill or repel insects? How effective are these foods? Are they specific for one insect?

2. How effective are plants such as marigolds as an insecticide? Do they repel or kill insects?

Project 3

How Effective Are Sun Shadows for Telling Time?

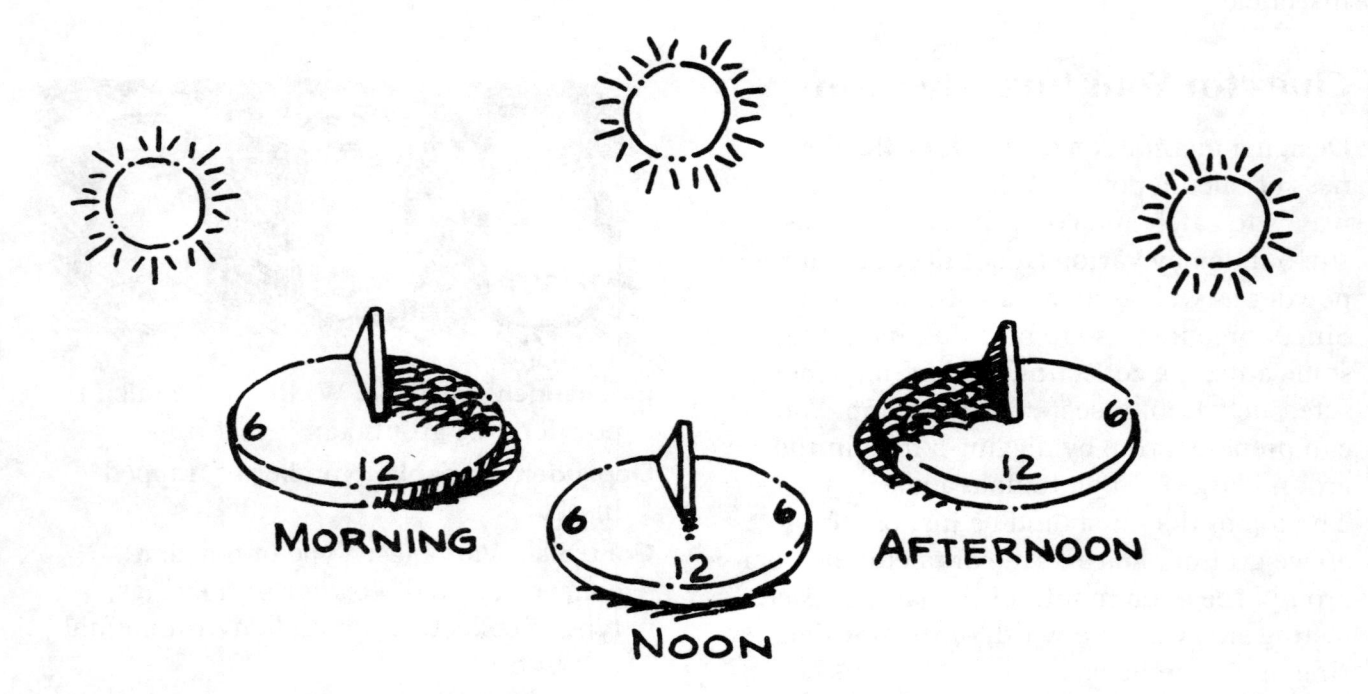

Category: Astronomy—Celestial Motion
Project Idea by: **Olivia Anderson**

Since the earliest recorded history, people have used the movement of celestial bodies (the natural things in the sky, such as stars, suns, moons, and planets) to tell time. The Sun was used most often because it is the easiest to follow. Earth's **rotation** (turning on an **axis**—an imaginary line through the center of an object around which the object rotates) each day makes the Sun appear to move across the sky. As Earth rotates, the Sun appears to rise above the eastern **horizon** (where the sky appears to touch Earth) in the morning, travel across the sky, and set below the western horizon in the evening.

The Sun's apparent motion from east to west across the sky causes objects on Earth to cast shadows. The changing position of the shadow cast by an object during the day indicates a change in time. The **sundial** is one of the oldest, if not the oldest, known device for the measurement of time. It is made of an object called a **gnomon**, which casts a shadow on a scaled surface. The shadow of the gnomon falls on different points on the scale, telling you what time it is.

The scale of a sundial is designed so that the differences in the direction of shadows during the day indicate time. In the morning, shadows are long and point toward the west.

As the day progresses, shadows shorten. At noon, when the Sun is at its highest point in the sky, shadows are shortest. In the afternoon, shadows are longer again and in the opposite direction, toward the east.

Not only does Earth rotate (turn on its axis), but it also **revolves** (to move in a curved path around another object) around the Sun. This motion changes the position of the Sun in the sky. In the **Northern Hemisphere** (the part of Earth north of the **equator**—the imaginary line dividing Earth into two parts), the Sun's highest noon position in the southern sky is on the first day of summer, called the **summer solstice** (the first day of summer on or about June 21/June 22). The Sun's lowest noon position during the year is on the first day of winter, called the **winter solstice** (the first day of winter on or about December 21/December 22). A project question might be, "How effective are Sun shadows for telling time?"

Clues for Your Investigation

Design a method for creating a time scale using shadows. One way is to use a watch to determine specific times during the day and to place objects such as stones on the ground to mark the position of shadows from a specific object at these times. Use the shadow of a stationary object such as a pole in an open area. Determine the time from the shadows from day to day for a specific time period such as each hour from 9 A.M. to 3 P.M. Check the accuracy against your watch. The longer the testing period, the more accurate the results.

9:00 AM

Independent Variable: Changing position of the Sun's zenith in the sky

Dependent Variable: Time measured by shadows

Controlled Variables: Testing materials—objects casting the shadows, shadow markers (stones), and the watch you use

Control: Time for the shadows marked on the first day of the investigation

Other Questions to Explore

1. What is latitude, and how does it affect the construction of a sundial?
2. What is the declination of the Sun, and should it be considered when constructing a sundial?
3. What is an analemmatic sundial, and how does its accuracy compare to a traditional sundial?

Project 4

How Does Earth's Rotation Affect the Position of the "Man in the Moon"?

Category: **Astronomy–Earth's Natural Satellite**
Project Idea by: **Leah Roldan**

A degree (°) is a unit that can be used to measure all or part of the distance around a circle. The distance around a full circle is 360°, a half circle is 180°, one-fourth of a circle is 90°, and so on. Each day, 24 hours, Earth rotates once; that is, Earth spins once around an imaginary line running through it called an axis. Earth would be turning in a counterclockwise direction if viewed from above the North Pole. You can calculate the number of degrees Earth rotates each hour by dividing 360° by 24 hours: 360° ÷ 24 hours = 15°/hour.

When two observers on Earth, one in the Northern Hemisphere and one in the Southern Hemisphere, view the night sky, the Southern Hemisphere observer sees the constellations and even the Moon in an upside-down position as compared to how they appear to the observer in the Northern Hemisphere. This is because the observers are viewing the celestial bodies from different directions. A similar thing would happen if you were on your back on a merry-go-round rotating in a counterclockwise direction and looked up at the sky. As you turned, the clouds in the sky would appear to be turning in a clockwise direction.

The dark places on a full Moon are commonly called the "Man in the Moon." If

Earth rotates 15° every hour in a counterclockwise direction, do celestial bodies appear to rotate the same amount in a clockwise direction? A project question might be "How does Earth's rotation affect the position of the 'Man in the Moon' as seen from Earth?"

Clues for Your Investigation

Determine a way to measure any circular motion of the "Man in the Moon" in degrees. For example, draw a circle for each observation. With a protractor, mark each 15° around its edge, starting with 0° at the top of the circle. Observe a full Moon, starting as early in the evening as possible. In one of the circles, make a sketch of the "Man in the Moon." Each hour, for 3 or more hours, make circle drawings of the "Man in the Moon."

MAN IN THE MOON

Independent Variable: Earth's rotation, measured in time

Dependent Variable: Position of the "Man in the Moon"

Controlled Variables: Moon, position of observation

Control: Position of the "Man in the Moon" during the first observation

Other Questions to Explore

1. How does Earth's rotation affect the position of stars in a constellation during the night?

2. What is a circumpolar star, and how does the latitude of the observer affect whether a star is circumpolar?

3. How does the revolution of Earth about the Sun affect the visible constellations?

Project 5

What Effect Does a Glucose Solution Have on the Longevity of Cut Flowers?

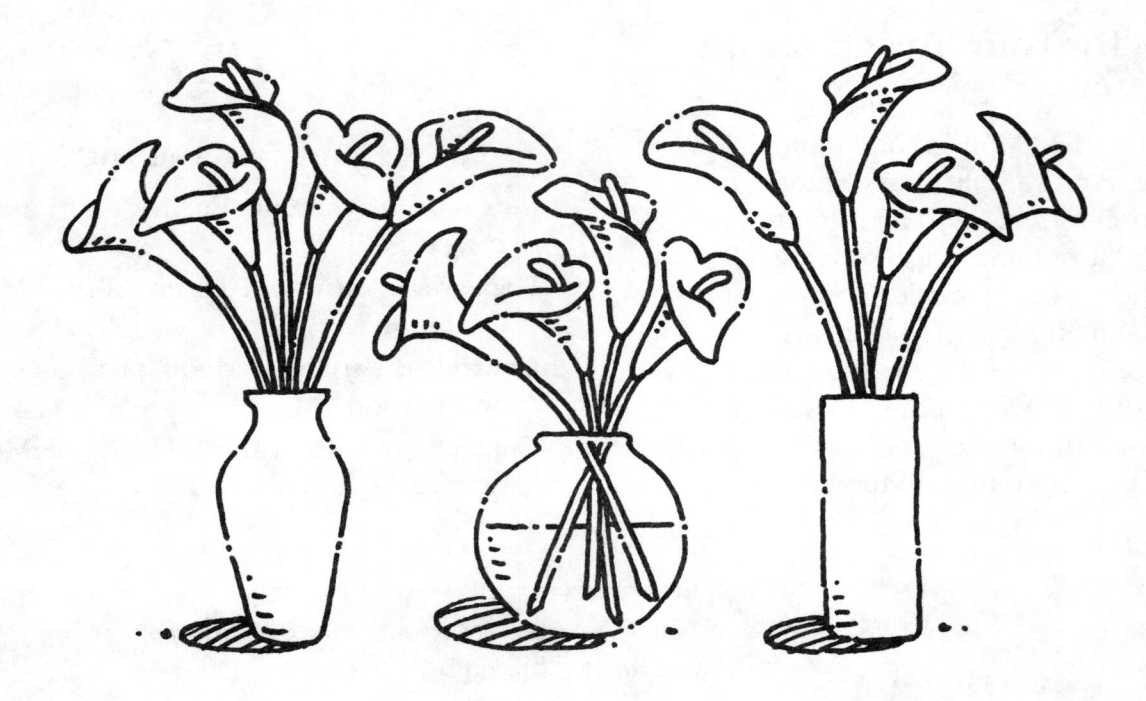

Category: **Biology—Botany—Anatomy**
Project Idea by: **Connor Janeski**

Plants produce their own food, mainly in their leaves, by a process called **photosynthesis**. This food-making process uses light, a form of radiant energy, to change **carbon dioxide** gas and water into oxygen and **glucose** (a type of sugar needed by plants and animals). Plants can change the sugar into energy, which can be used for all plant processes necessary for life and growth.

Plants have tube-shaped structures called xylem that carry sap from the roots to other parts of the plant. **Sap** is a liquid **solution** (a mixture of a liquid with substances dissolved in it) containing nutrients including glucose. When the stem connected to a flower is cut, sap can continue to move through the xylem if the cut end is placed in a liquid. The **longevity** (the length of life) of a cut flower depends on several things, one being the continued movement of sap to the flower. Without sap, cut flowers will **wilt** (become limp or droopy). Since plants need glucose to make energy, a project question might be, "What effect does a glucose solution have on the longevity of cut flowers?"

Clues for Your Investigation

Often, a cut flower quickly dies because **microbes** (organisms that are too small to be seen with the unaided eye) multiply and form a plug in the end of the cut stems, blocking sap from moving through the xylem. To increase the longevity of cut flowers, it is important to use clean cutting tools and containers, which helps control the growth of stem-plugging microbes. Cutting the stems while holding them under water prevents air bubbles from plugging the stems. Use the same kind of flowers and the same cutting tools and procedure to collect or to prepare purchased flowers.

A source of glucose is white corn syrup. Decide on the amount of syrup that will be used for each test and mix it with distilled water. Put several flowers in a vase or jar containing a different amount of glucose and one with no glucose (the control). Design a method of measuring the longevity of a cut flower. For example, the flower will be considered dead when any part of its petals change color.

Independent Variable: Amount of glucose

Dependent Variable: Longevity of cut flowers

Controlled Variables: Type of flower, how the flower is cut, cutting tools, containers, distilled water, environmental conditions

Control: Distilled water—no glucose

Other Questions to Explore

How would these variables affect the longevity of cut flowers: (1) Water temperature, (2) tap water instead of distilled water, and (3) table sugar instead of corn syrup?

Project 6

What Effect Does the Color of Light Have on Phototropism?

Category: **Biology—Botany—Behaviorism**
Project Idea by: **Vincent Daigger and Evan Filion**

Tropism is the movement of organisms in response to a stimulus such as food, light, or water. **Stimuli** are things that temporarily excite or quicken a response in an organism. **Positive tropism** is movement toward the stimulus, and **negative tropism** is movement away from the stimulus. Plant motion is due to inside pressure and unequal growth.

Phototropism is the movement of organisms in response to light. In plant phototropism, the plant bends toward the light. The bending happens because of unequal growth on the sides of the plant stem. The part of the stem exposed to light grows more slowly than the part not exposed. Because of the difference in the stem length on the two sides, the plant bends toward the shorter, sun-exposed side. **Auxin** is a light-sensitive growth chemical. When a plant is exposed to light, auxin concentrates on the dark side. This results in the dark side growing faster.

Visible light is a type of **radiant energy** (energy in the form of waves that can travel through space) that can be seen by the human eye. **White light** is a combination of all light colors in the **visible spectrum**, which in order from least to most energy are red, yellow, orange, green, blue, indigo, and violet. Sunlight and light from lightbulbs are examples of white light. A project question might be, "What effect does the color of light have on phototropism?"

Clues for Your Investigation

When white light passes through a colored, transparent piece of plastic, some of its colors are absorbed and others pass through. The colored plastic is said to filter out colors. For example, a red piece of plastic will filter out all but red light, which passes through.

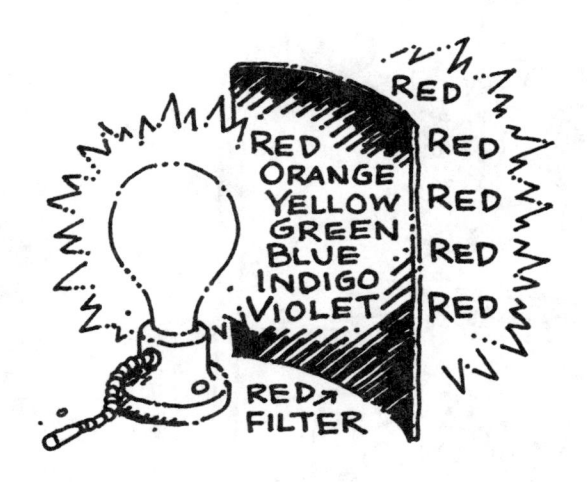

Design a testing method using filters to test the effect of different-colored lights on phototropism. One way might be to prepare a cardboard box with two 1-inch (2 cm) holes on opposite sides. Leave one hole uncovered so that white light enters. Cover the other hole with colored, transparent plastic such as red, green, yellow, or blue.

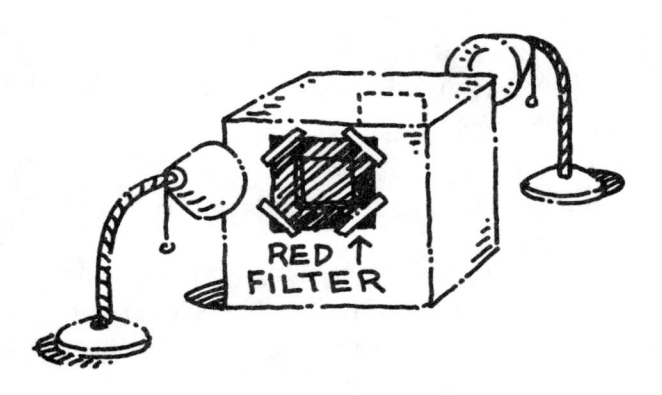

Place the box over a testing plant. The box and plant should be in a position so that equal amounts of light enter both openings. This can be done by placing the box in a darkened room with one lamp on either side of the box. Keep the testing plant moist with water. Without disturbing the position of the plant, raise the box each day for seven or more days and observe any change in the direction of the plant leaves. Repeat the procedure with different-colored plastic covering one of the holes of the testing box. Determine how to measure the amount of phototropism. You may wish to take photographs and compare them to determine any change in position of the leaves.

Independent Variable: Light color
Dependent Variable: Amount of phototropism
Controlled Variables: Type of plants, testing procedure, method of measuring phototropism, time of exposure
Control: White light

Other Questions to Explore

1. What effect does the time of exposure have on phototropism?
2. What effect does the type of plant have on phototropism?
3. Plants placed in a maze will grow toward light. What effect does the distance between the plant and the light opening have on the plant's phototropic response?

Project 7

What Effect Does the Position of Artificial Light Have on Plant Growth?

Category: **Biology—Botany—Physiology**

Project Idea by: **David Murphy**

Light is necessary for healthy plant growth. The process by which plants use light energy, water, and carbon dioxide to make food is called photosynthesis. Photosynthesis occurs in plants that have **chlorophyll**, which is a green chemical that can capture light energy.

Plants must have all the light colors in the visible spectrum to grow properly. Some of the light colors promote stem growth, flowering, leaf formation, and dark green foliage. The blue and red parts of the visible spectrum are most important for photosynthesis.

Artificial light is light from a man-made source. Indoor plants that don't get enough sunlight can survive well with white artificial light. Indoor lighting can be placed in different positions in relation to the plants. For example, for a dramatic display, lighting might be placed above and/or beneath plants. A project question might be, "What effect does the position of artificial light have on plant growth?"

Clues for Your Investigation

Design a method for exposing plants to artificial light from different directions: overhead, beneath, and to the side. For example, plants can be placed in separate boxes so that the only light received is from an opening in the box. The testing should be in an unlit room or one as dark as possible so that most or all of the light comes from the testing lamps. All plants should be exposed to light for the same amount of time. Design a method for measuring plant growth. You may wish to start with seeds. After sprouts appear above the soil, begin measuring plant growth by measuring the length of the stems. Since sunlight basically comes from above plants, the light from above the plants can arbitrarily be selected as the control.

Independent Variable: Direction of light

Dependent Variable: Plant growth—length of stems

Controlled Variables: Testing method; measuring method; type of plants, potting soil, containers, and environmental conditions; types and wattage of light bulbs; amount of light exposure; distance of light from the plants

Control: Arbitrarily selected light from above

Other Questions to Explore

1. What effect do different types of artificial light have on plant growth?
2. What effect do grow lamps have on plant growth?

Project 8

How Does Exposure Time to Microwaves Affect Seed Germination?

Category: **Biology—Botany—Physiology**
Project Idea by: **Lynsie and Jacob Connor**

One way that plants produce other plants is by seeds. The **sprouting** (to begin to grow) of seeds is called **germination**. During germination the **embryo** (an organism's earliest stage of development) develops. The embryo looks like a baby plant, and it breaks out of the seed when it grows. The embryo needs nutrients to grow. The part of the seed where the nutrients are stored is called the **cotyledon**. As the baby plant (embryo) begins to grow, part of it grows down and part of it grows up. The downward-growing part forms a **root system**, which anchors the plant in the ground and takes in water and nutrients from the soil. The upward-growing part of the embryo contains the **shoot system**, which forms all the parts of the plant that are generally above ground, including the stems and leaves.

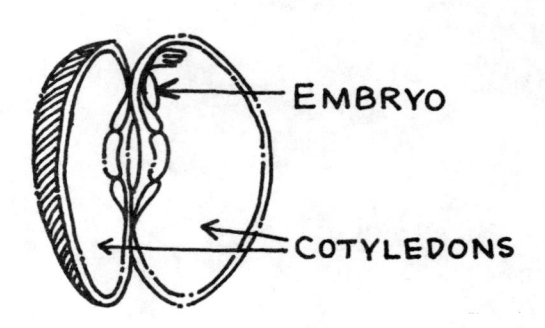

Microwaves are a high energy type of radiant energy. Microwaves are absorbed by some materials such as water and fat in foods, causing the material to get hot. But microwaves pass through other materials such as paper plates. In a microwave oven, the microwaves cause water and fat molecules in food to flip back and forth. The moving molecules bounce into one another. Much like quickly rubbing your hands together causes them to feel hot, the friction of the molecules bouncing into one another causes food cooked in microwave ovens to get hot.

Microwaves have been used to kill the embryos in birdseed so that seeds that scatter or pass through the birds do not germinate and produce weeds (unwanted plants). Will any amount of microwaves kill seeds? A project question might be "How does exposure time to microwaves affect seed germination?"

Clues for Your Investigation

CAUTION: Adult supervision is needed when using a microwave oven.

Some seeds, such as pinto beans and radish seeds, grow quickly. Select one type of seed. Place an equal number of the seeds on paper towels in the microwave for different intervals of time, such as 5, 10, 20, and 30 seconds. CAUTION: In some ovens the magnetron tube producing the microwaves can be damaged by unabsorbed energy. Since seeds may not absorb all the microwaves produced, place a cup of water in the oven to absorb the energy so that the oven does not get damaged. After all the seeds have been microwaved, plant them in soil in separate containers. Plant all seeds the same depth. For a control, plant seeds that have not been microwaved. The time it takes from planting a seed to the first signs of growth can be called the **germination starting time (GST)**. The time it takes from planting a seed to the end of germination can be called the **germination time (GT)**. Determine the GT for your project experiment. For example, the GT could be the time it takes for the shoot to break through the soil. Compare the germination times of the different batches of seeds.

Independent Variable: Exposure time to microwaves

Dependent Variable: Germination time

Controlled Variables: Type of seed, type of soil, containers, watering procedure for each plant, environmental conditions such as temperature, humidity, and light

Control: Seeds that have not been placed in the microwave oven

Other Questions to Explore

1. What effect do microwaves have on different types of seeds?
2. What effect does microwaved soil have on seed germination?

Project 9

What Effect Does the Size of a Plant's Leaves Have on the Plant's Transpiration Rate?

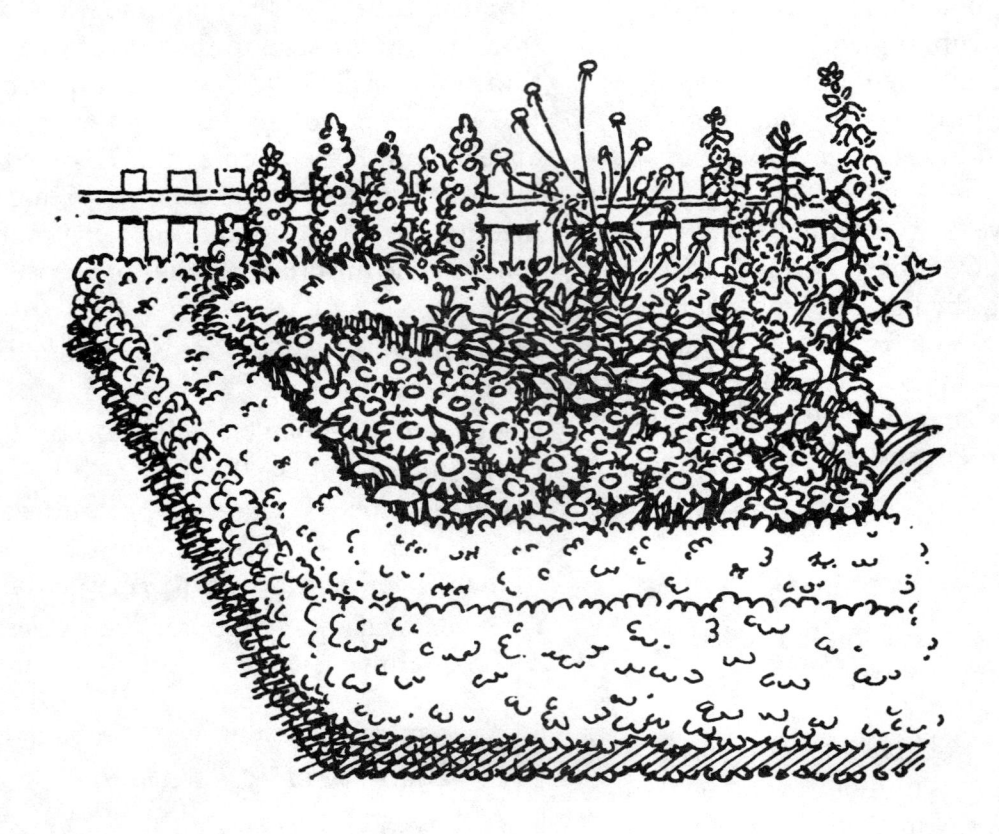

Category: **Biology—Botany—Physiology**
Project Idea by: **Jonna Butcher**

The process by which plants lose water by vaporization (the change from a liquid to a gas) is called **transpiration**. The water escapes in gas form from the plant through **stomata**, which are special openings in the outer layer of plants, generally in the leaves. (The singular form of *stomata* is *stoma*.) The stomata can be opened or closed by **guard cells**.

As particles of water that move out of the plant through the stomata are lost by vaporization at the surface of leaves, more water enters the plants through the roots and fills the space left by the lost water particles. If the water lost by transpiration is not replaced by water from the soil, there is a loss of **turgor** (the pressure within plant cells) and the stomata close. With enough loss of turgor, the plant wilts (becomes limp and droopy).

Transpiration rate is the amount of water

lost by a plant in a specific period of time. A project question might be, "What effect does the size of a plant's leaves have on its transpiration rate?"

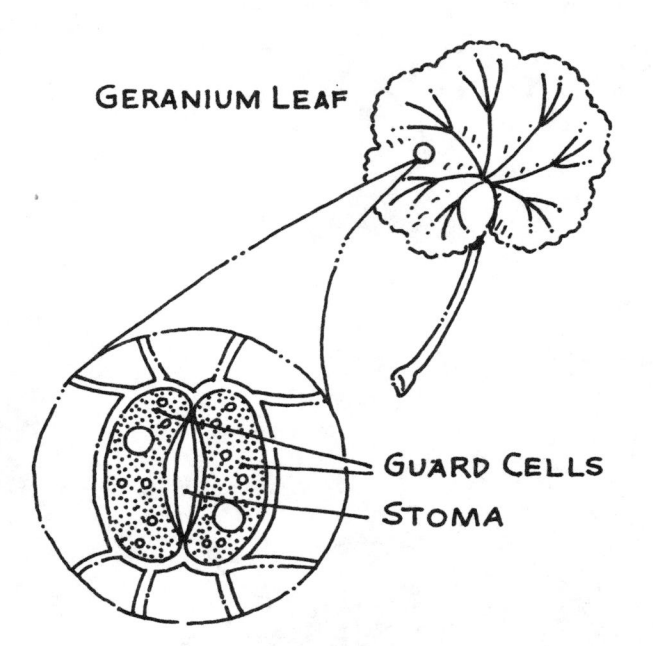

Geranium Leaf
Guard Cells
Stoma

Clues for Your Investigation

Capture the water lost by transpiration from the leaves of plants with different-sized leaves. One way is to cover the leaves with a plastic bag and measure the water collected in the bag after a specific amount of time. To make sure the environmental conditions are the same for each testing, select plants near one another and do the testing at the same time.

Independent Variable: Leaf size

Dependent Variable: Transpiration rate

Controlled Variables: Number of leaves in each collection bag, type of bag, how the bag is secured to the plant, time of testing, environmental conditions

Control: Arbitrarily selected plant with medium-sized leaves

Other Questions to Explore

1. How does temperature affect transpiration?
2. What effect does humidity have on transpiration?
3. How does the amount of light received by a plant affect transpiration?

Project 10

How Do Seasonal Color Changes in the Environment Affect Camouflage in Animals?

Category: **Biology—Ecology**
Project Idea by: **Tyler Halpern**

Camouflage is a disguise caused by similarities between the colors and patterns of an animal's body and those found in its environment. Animals with colors that blend in with their background are said to be camouflaged. Camouflage protects animals from **predators** (animals that kill and eat other animals). For example, a bird that feeds on grasshoppers will have trouble spotting a green grasshopper on green grass. Coloring that helps to camouflage an animal from a predator is called **protective coloration**.

Earth's temperate zones include most of North America, Europe, Asia, and the southern parts of South America, Africa, and Australia. In the temperate zones, there are four divisions of the year called **climatic seasons** (divisions of the year based on average temperature and the amount of time that the Sun is in the sky each day): winter, spring, summer, and autumn. **Winter** has the shortest days, meaning that the Sun is in the sky for the least amount of time each day. Winter also has the coldest days. Generally, there are few green plants in the winter. Most leaves are dead and more brown in color.

Spring follows winter with medium-length cool days. This is the most colorful season. Following spring the days get longer and warmer, leading into **summer**, with the longest and hottest days. Summer begins with very colorful plants. As summer progresses, the colors remain if the rainfall is good. Without rain many green grasses die and turn yellow or brown. **Autumn** follows summer. Like spring, autumn has medium-length cool days. Each day of this season gets shorter and colder, leading to winter, when the cycle begins again. During autumn, leaves no longer produce **pigment** (some substances that provide color to a material). Without chlorophyll, the green pigment that disappears first, the yellow and orange pigments in the leaves can be seen for a time. Low temperatures and bright sunshine encourage the production of a red pigment for a time. A project question might be "How do seasonal color changes in the environment affect camouflage in animals?"

Clues for Your Investigation

Determine how seasonal changes in the color of ground cover affect which insect color is most camouflaged. Use colored bread pieces to represent insects. Ask an adult to prepare the bread pieces by trimming off the crust, then cutting each piece of bread into pieces of equal size. Soak the bread in different-colored water solutions made by mixing ¼ cup (63 mL) water with 10 drops of food coloring. Use different colors such as red, yellow, and green. White can be the control. Soak the white bread pieces in water with no coloring so that they have the same texture as the colored pieces when dry. Since it can take 3 or more weeks for birds to find a new feeding area, you may wish to offer birdseed for a period of time until the birds start to regularly visit your testing area.

Independent Variable: Seasonal ground color changes

Dependent Variable: Number of each color of bread pieces eaten by birds

Controlled Variables: Same type, size, and number of bread pieces of each color for each testing, equal testing times, same time of day, same testing location

Control: Uncolored bread pieces

Other Questions to Explore

1. What effect does surface type have on camouflage?
2. What effect do patterns have on camouflage?
3. What effect does light have on camouflage?

Project 11

How Does the Amount of Water in a Gel Affect Its Flexibility?

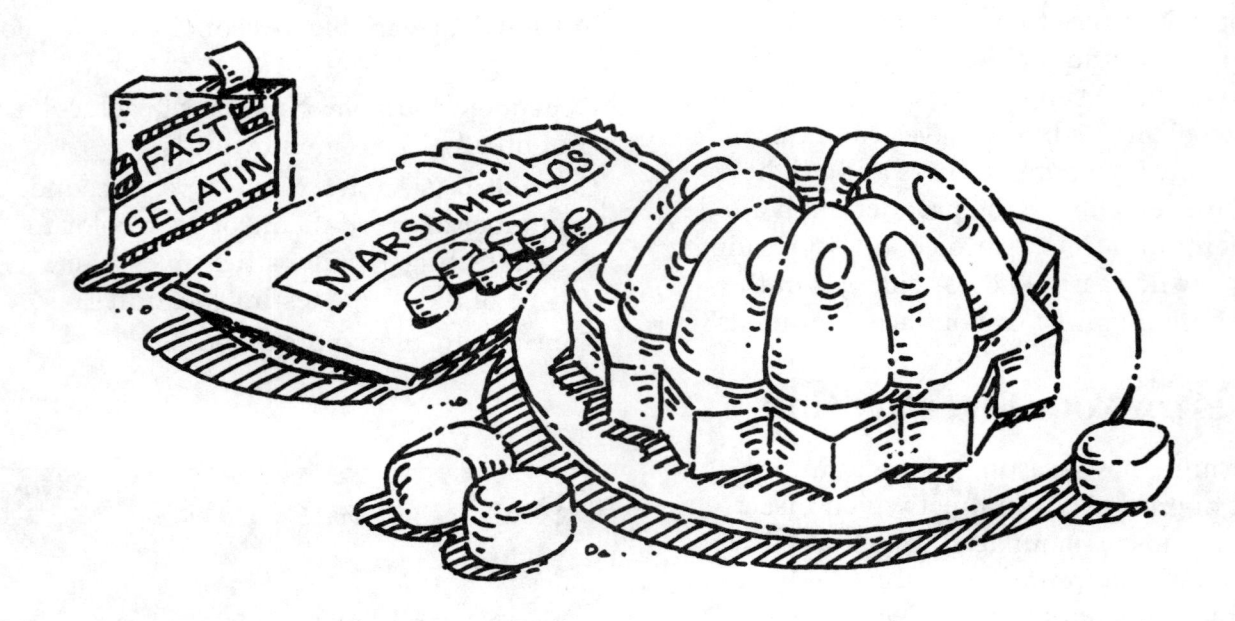

Category: **Biology—Food Science**
Project Idea by: **Benjamin Skrabanek**

Gelatin is a substance made of animal protein. **Proteins** are nutrients made of one or more chains of chemicals. The protein chains forming gelatin are like long, tangled strands of sticky spaghetti. Gelatin is flavored and colored to make jiggly desserts and is also used in marshmallows and other foods.

When gelatin is mixed with hot water, the protein chains separate from one another and can freely move about. As the mixture cools, the proteins begin to recombine by forming **bonds** (the forces that hold chemicals together) between the chains. The chains connect in a haphazard way, forming a tangled web in which water in the mixture is trapped. This process is called **gelling**, and the semisolid that is formed is called a **gel**. The protein web of the gel gives it shape, and the trapped water causes it to be **flexible** (able to change its shape in response to a force, then recover its original shape when the force is removed); that is, the gel can jiggle. A project problem might be, "How does the amount of water in a gel affect its flexibility?"

Clues for Your Investigation

With adult help, follow the basic directions on a package of dessert gelatin. Make changes only in the amount of water mixed into the dry gelatin for each testing. Keep the amount of gelatin the same and vary only the amount of water for several different gels. Create a scale for testing the flexibility of the gels. For example, shake the gels after they have cooled, and determine on a scale of 1 to 10, with 1 being the least flexible, how easily they return to their original shape.

Independent Variable: Amount of water

Dependent Variable: Flexibility of gel

Controlled Variables: Type of dessert gelatin, amount of dry gelatin used, temperature of water, cooling time, testing procedure for flexibility

Control: Gel made with the median amount of water

Other Questions to Explore

1. What effect do additives such as flavorings or sugar have on the flexibility of a gel?

2. What effect does the addition of fresh fruit have on the ability of a gelatin to gel? Canned fruit? Types of fruit—citrus or noncitrus?

Project 12

What Effect Does the Type of Flour Have on the Ability of Calcium Propionate to Inhibit Bread Mold?

Category: **Biology—Food Science**
Project Idea by: **Alana Davicino and Arielle Lewen**

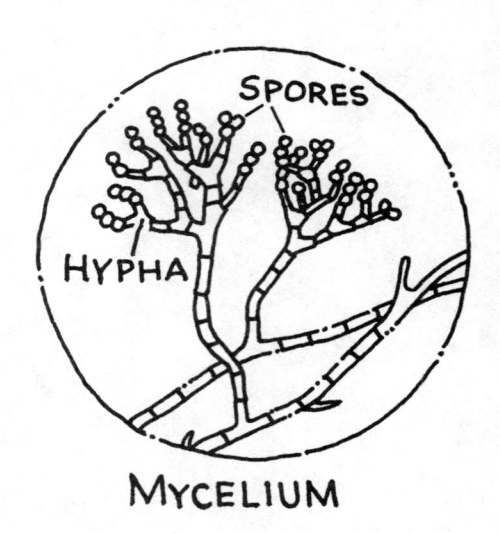

Fungi are single-celled or multicellular organisms that obtain food by the direct absorption of nutrients. Fungi include such things as mushrooms, athlete's foot, and mold. **Mold** is a fungus that produces a fuzzy, cobweblike growth on moist materials, including food. Black bread mold, *Aspergillus niger*, is one of the most familiar molds. This mold begins as a microscopic, airborne **spore** (a reproductive cell) that germinates (begins to grow) on contact with the moist surface of a food source, such as bread. It spreads rapidly, forming a netlike mass called **mycelia** (fungal bodies). Mycelia are tangled masses of threadlike structures called **hyphae**. (The singular form of *mycelia* is *mycelium*.) Spores are produced at the top of hyphae. The spores are stored in cases. When the cases break, hundreds of spores that are small and easily carried by any air movement are released. If the spores land in a suitable place, they grow and the cycle begins again.

Molds must have a warm, moist environment, oxygen, some light, and food to produce their spores. Most molds grow well on starchy foods (bread), the rind of some fruit (lemons and oranges), and materials high in cellulose, such as wood, hay, and paper products such as cardboard.

Food preservatives, such as calcium propionate in breads, inhibit the growth of mold. Breads are made from different kinds of flour, including rye, wheat, and corn. A project question might be, "What effect does the type of flour have on the ability of calcium propionate to inhibit bread mold?"

Clues for Your Investigation

Design a method of testing different kinds of bread made with different kinds of flour. All the breads should have the mold-inhibiting additive calcium propionate. The most common bread is made with white flour, so you could use this as a control. One way of testing the bread is to place a moistened paper towel inside a 1-gallon plastic resealable bag. Cut equal-sized pieces of each of the types of bread and place them side by side on top of the moistened paper inside the plastic bag. Close the bag and seal it with tape to prevent the bag from being accidentally opened. Use a marking pen to write the bread type above each bread piece on the outside of the plastic bag. Repeat this procedure, preparing four or more additional bags. Keep the bags at room temperature for two weeks or until each bread piece has mold. Using a magnifying lens, observe the surface of each bread piece daily by looking through the plastic. Determine when the bread will be considered to have mold such as the first sign of black hyphae. CAUTION: Do not do this project if you are allergic to mold. Even if you are not allergic, leave containers with mold closed so that you do not breathe in an excessive number of spores. Discard the closed containers when the project is finished.

Independent Variable: Types of bread flour
Dependent Variable: Growth of bread mold
Controlled Variables: Type of preservative, testing procedure, containers, temperature, size of bread pieces, environmental conditions
Control: White bread

Other Questions to Explore

1. What effect does temperature have on mold growth?
2. What effect does water have on mold growth?
3. What effect does the type of food have on mold growth?
4. What is pH and how does it affect mold growth?
5. Are there natural ingredients that inhibit mold growth? If so, how effective are they?

Project 13

What Effect Does Light Have on the Rate of Planaria Regeneration?

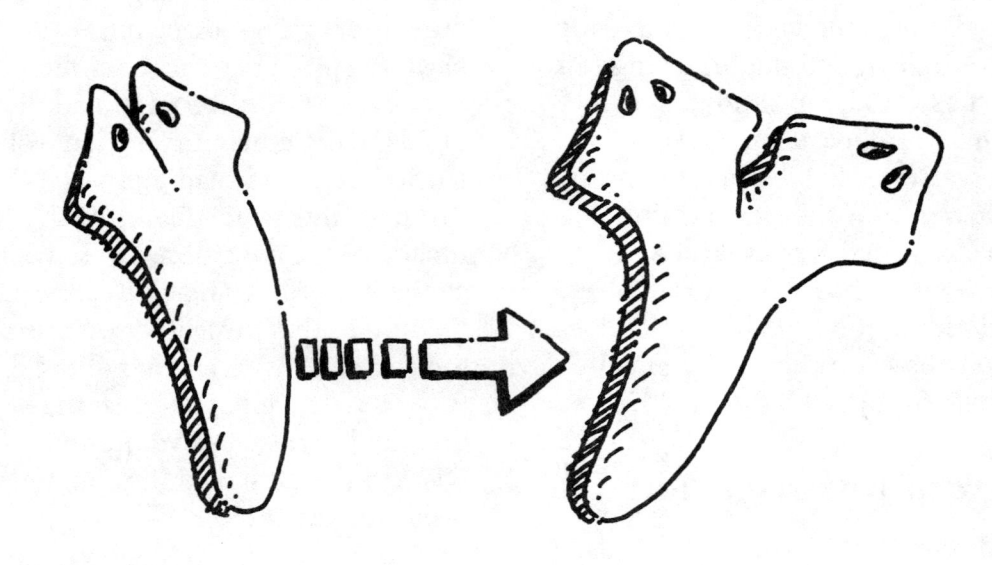

Category: **Biology—Reproduction**
Project Idea by: **Evan Sunshine and Christopher Wenz**

Regeneration is the growth of new tissue or parts of an organism that have been lost or destroyed. Regeneration is a form of asexual reproduction in which a new organism is formed from one parent. Some animals, generally **invertebrates** (animals without backbones) such as planaria, can regenerate a complete body from small fragments of themselves. Planaria are flatworms found in freshwater such as weedy ponds, slow-moving streams, and small creeks.

Planaria regenerate from small parts cut from their bodies. For example, if a planaria's head is cut off, the beheaded body grows a new head and the separated head grows a new body. Within about 15 minutes after amputation, the cut edges are covered by **epithelial cells** (cells on the surface of organisms). Within about five days, distinct new parts are seen on each cut surface. A project question might be, "What effect does light have on the rate of planaria regeneration?"

Clues for Your Investigation

Planaria can be purchased from scientific catalog supply companies. Ask your teacher to order these for you. The company should also give you information about keeping the planaria alive, as well as clues on the safest way of handling, how to cut them, and how to dispose of them after the experiment. When cutting, ask for assistance from an adult. One way to help keep the planaria immobile while you work on them is to place them on an ice cube. The cut parts must be kept in pond water or a freshwater aquarium. Prepare four or more containers of cut planaria and place each container in an area receiving a different amount of light. The container in the dark will be the control. Observe the cut parts each day for two or more weeks.

Independent Variable: Amount of light
Dependent Variable: Rate of regeneration
Controlled Variables: Testing procedure, how planaria are cut, containers, temperature, environmental conditions
Control: Planaria with no light

Other Questions to Explore

1. What effect would temperature have on regeneration of planaria?
2. Is there a size limit on the pieces of planaria that will regenerate into complete new organisms?
3. What effect does the direction of the cut have on planaria regeneration?

Project 14

What Effect Does Regular Physical Exercise Have on the Lungs' Vital Capacity?

Category: **Biology—Zoology—Anatomy**
Project Idea by: **Robert Ali**

Lungs are balloonlike structures in the chest that are used to exchange oxygen and carbon dioxide between your blood and the atmosphere. As you **inhale** (breathe in), air is drawn into your lungs. As you **exhale** (breathe out), you expel gases from your lungs. In the lungs, oxygen from inhaled air moves into your **blood** (the liquid in animals that carries nutrients and oxygen to cells and takes away wastes) and is carried to the cells throughout the body to produce energy. Also in the lungs, **carbon dioxide** (a gaseous waste) leaves the blood and enters tubes, then is expelled when you exhale. The breathing rate of a healthy adult at rest is about 12 times a minute. A baby's breathing rate is about 24 times a minute.

Normally, you breathe through your nose. Air enters the nose and moves down the back of the **pharynx** (the throat), where it enters the **trachea** (the breathing tube). At the end of the trachea, the passage splits to form two tubes called **bronchi** that lead to the lungs. In the lungs, each bronchus divides many times, forming small tubes called **bronchioles**. At the end of each bronchiole is a balloon-shaped structure called an **alviolus** (air sac). The lungs contain millions of alvioli, and around each are many capillaries. A **capillary** is the body's smallest blood vessel. Through the capillaries, oxygen from inhaled air is transferred to the blood, and waste from the blood is transferred to the lungs before being exhaled.

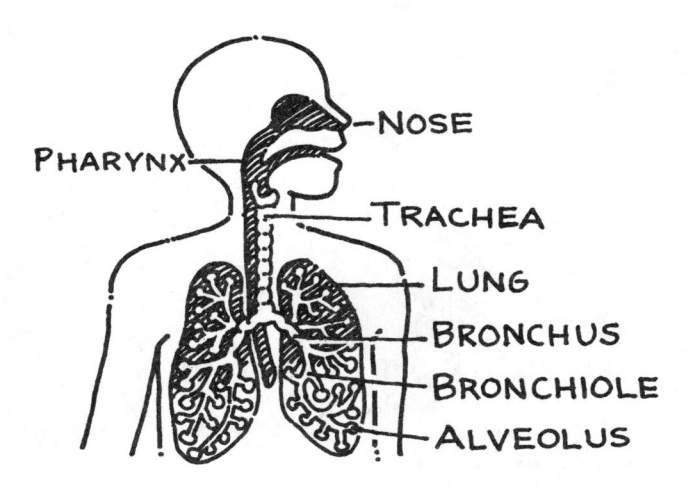

Diagram labels: Pharynx, Nose, Trachea, Lung, Bronchus, Bronchiole, Alveolus

When the lungs are filled, they can hold varying amounts of air depending on the size of the person. **Tidal air** is the amount of air involved during normal, relaxed inhaling and exhaling. **Vital capacity** of the lungs is the largest amount of air that can be exhaled after taking a deep breath. A project question might be, "What effect does regular physical exercise have on the lungs' vital capacity?"

Clues for Your Investigation

Test the vital lung capacity of several people in two groups: one group of people who are athletic and one group of people who are not athletic. People in both groups should be the same gender and age and of a similar size. Each person should stand, take a deep breath, then blow up a balloon with a single breath and tie a knot in the balloon. The sizes of the blown-up balloons will be compared to indicate vital lung capacity. Design a way to measure the size of each balloon such as measuring around the balloons with a flexible measuring tape. An increase in balloon size indicates an increase in vital lung capacity.

Independent Variable: Physical fitness
Dependent Variables: Sizes of the inflated balloons
Controlled Variables: Age, gender, and size of subject; type of balloon; position of subject (standing, sitting, etc.)
Control: Lung vital capacity with no exercise

Other Questions to Explore

1. Does age affect vital capacity?
2. How does the lungs' tidal volume compare to vital capacity?
3. How does the lungs' reserve air compare to vital capacity?

Project 15

What Effect Does Gender Have on the Stroop Test Color Recognition Response Time?

Category: **Biology—Zoology—Behavior**

Project Idea by: **Kayla Miklas and Rachel Orfinger**

The American psychologist John Ridley Stroop (1897–1973) devised a test in 1935 called the **Stroop test**. This test demonstrates the interference that happens in the brain when two simultaneous thinking process are involved, such as reading words and identifying colors. In this test, participants see the names of colors printed in ink that is the same color named by the word as well as in other colors. For example, the word *red* could be written with red or green ink. The participants are asked to identify the print color. When the print color is different from the color word, participants usually take longer to name the print color and often say the color word first instead of saying the name of the print color.

Skills such as reading that are highly practiced become automatic and can be carried out with little or no mental effort. In fact, the longer you practice reading, the more difficult it is not to read words you see. It takes considerable mental effort not to read them.

Reading and identifying colors are two separate mental tasks. But since a person tends to automatically read printed words, it is easier for that person to read a word than to name a color.

The mental process involved in reading and naming a color is called **inhibition**, which means you stop one brain response in order for another response to be processed. There are two possible responses in the Stroop test: reading a printed word and naming the color in which the word is printed. Since reading is more of an automatic response, to identify the color in which the word is printed, you have to inhibit your response to read the word.

Do boys and girls of the same age inhibit reading and recognize color at the same speed? A project question might be, "What effect does gender have on the Stroop test color recognition response time?"

Clues for Your Investigation

Prepare two reading lists. In the first, write the names of colors in the color indicated by the name. In the second list, write the same names in a color different from each name. Select a group of boys and girls of the same age to be tested. Test each separately. Give each person these instructions: "Do not read the words. Instead, identify the color of the print." Time how long it takes each person to recognize the color of each word.

Independent Variable: Gender

Dependent Variable: Time it takes to recognize colors

Controlled Variables: Same words, size of words, environmental conditions, age of participants

Control: List of words where the name of the color is printed in that color

---

Other Questions to Explore

1. What effect would non-color-related words such as *dog*, *cat*, *bird*, and *hamburger* have on the Stroop test?
2. What effect would testing a young child who cannot read have on the results of the Stroop test?
3. What effect does age have on the Stroop test?

Project 16

How Does the Volume of Background Music Affect Short-Term Memory?

Category: **Biology—Behavioral Science**
Project Idea by: **Laura Coiro and Nicole Fieger**

Memory is the ability to retain and recall past experiences. Memory is a **cognitive process**, which is the mental process a person uses for remembering, reasoning, understanding, problem solving, evaluating, and using judgment; that is, it is what a person knows and understands.

There are three basic types of memory: sensory, short-term, and long-term. **Sensory memory** is the ability to retain impressions of sensory information after the original stimulus has ceased. **Sensory information** includes what you discover by hearing, seeing, touching, tasting, and smelling. This memory is thought to last from 1 second to 2 seconds.

Short-term memory is your working memory; that is, it is your primary memory or active memory, the one you use most of the time. Short-term memory is like taking notes for temporary recall of the information being processed. For instance, in order to understand a sentence, the words you read are held in short-term memory. Information is either forgotten or transferred from your short-term memory to your long-term memory after about 30 seconds. **Long-term memory** is information that you can recall after days or even years.

Interference is one of the reasons that short-term information is forgotten. **Interference** means that information in storage is distorted as new information is stored. A project question might be, "How does volume of background music affect short-term memory?"

Clues for Your Investigation

Test four groups, each with a different volume of background music: low, medium, high, and as a control, no music. Design a short-term memory test such as having testers view six different cards with an increasing number of letters on them. For example, cards can have 2, 4, 6, 8, 10, and 12 letters written in capital letters in a straight line. Each card will be viewed for a specific length of time such as 3 seconds. Then the tester will write down as many letters as he or she remembers.

Independent Variable: Volume of music

Dependent Variable: Short-term memory

Controlled Variables: Type of music, testing conditions, age and gender of testers, size and color of letters

Control: No background music

Other Questions to Explore

1. What effect does age have on memory?
2. What effect does gender have on memory?
3. What is consolidation time and how does it affect memory?
4. What is distributed practice and how does it affect memory?

Project 17

How Does Color Intensity Affect the Perceived Sweetness of Food?

Category: **Biology—Zoology—Behavior**

Project Idea by: **Amanda Accardi and Jennifer Phelan**

You experience various tastes because of **taste buds**, which are special cells on your tongue and on the roof and the back of your mouth. Most of your taste buds are located on the tip, sides, and back of your tongue. While you have thousands of taste buds, they detect four main tastes: sweet, salty, sour, and bitter. Although all of the taste buds can detect more than one taste, each is best at detecting one of the primary tastes.

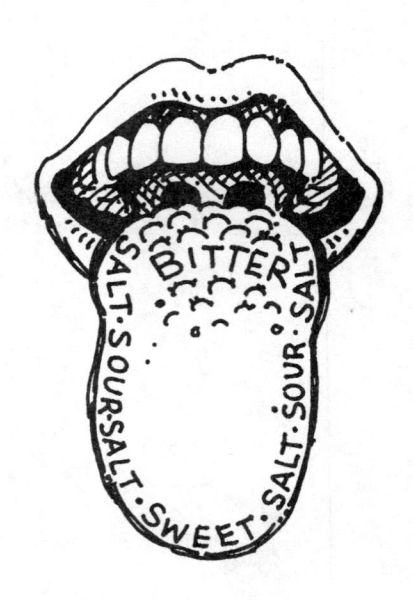

The taste buds for sweet are more concentrated on the tip of your tongue, for salt and sour along the sides, and for bitter at the back. Even though the different types of taste buds are more concentrated in some areas, there is quite a bit of overlap of the taste areas and much variation from one person to the next. The flavors of food that you eat are a combination of the four tastes of sweet, salty, sour, and bitter.

Your tongue is also sensitive to touch, cold, heat, and pain. Whether the food is wet or dry, soft or hard, smooth or lumpy, hot or cold makes a difference in how its taste is perceived. In addition, a food's taste depends on how it smells and looks. A project question might be, "How does color intensity affect the perceived sweetness of food?"

Clues for Your Investigation

Prepare cherry-flavored drinks that differ only in the amount of red food coloring. Ask a group of the same age range and gender to taste the drinks and determine which tastes the sweetest. After tasting one drink, each tester should drink a small amount of water to rinse the previous drink out of his or her mouth. Compare the results to determine what effect, if any, the amount of coloring has on the perceived flavor intensity.

Independent Variable: Color intensity

Dependent Variable: Sweetness of taste

Controlled Variables: Sweetness of each drink color, age of testers, gender of testers, testing conditions

Control: Drink with no sweetener

Other Questions to Explore

1. What effect, if any, does color have on the acceptability of a drink (how much people liked the drink)?
2. Would the age of the testing group affect the results?
3. Would the gender of the testing group affect the results?

Project 18

What Effect Does the Type of Video Game Have on Blood Pressure?

Category: **Biology—Zoology—Physiology**
Project Idea by: **Ryan William Brown**

The force of blood on the walls of the **arteries** (the blood vessels carrying blood from the heart to the body) is called **blood pressure**. Normal blood pressure for most adults is about 120/80. Your normal blood pressure may be different from the average. Only your doctor can determine what is normal for you. The first measurement is the blood pressure on the inside walls of the arteries when the heart contracts and pushes blood out. This is called **systolic pressure**. The second measurement is the blood pressure on the inside walls of the arteries when the heart is resting. This is called **diastolic pressure**.

If blood pressure is consistently higher than normal during a rest time, the condition is called **hypertension**. Hypertension can cause health problems such as heart attacks, strokes, and kidney problems. But it's normal for a person's blood pressure to increase during exercise or if the person is stressed or anxious. Would playing a violent or action-packed video game be enough to raise blood pressure? A project question might be, "What effect does the type of video game have on blood pressure?"

Clues for Your Investigation

Design a way to test the blood pressure of 20 or more different subjects before and after playing at least two different video games. Choose subjects of the same age and gender, and test them at the same time of day. Select a place where each subject will be tested with no distractions. Before the subjects play a selected video game, check their blood pressure using an automatic blood pressure machine. After they have played the game for a predetermined time such as 15 minutes, check their blood pressure again. After they have rested for a predetermined time—10 or more minutes—recheck their blood pressure. Then have each subject play a second video game that is not as violent as the first one. After playing the game, again check the subject's blood pressure.

Independent Variable: Type of video game

Dependent Variable: Blood pressure

Controlled Variables: Gender and age of subjects, time of testing, video games used for each subject, blood pressure testing method

Control: Blood pressure of subjects before playing video games

Other Questions to Explore

1. What effect does gender have on the results of the video game/blood pressure testing?
2. What effect does age have on the results of the video game/blood pressure testing?

Project 19

What Effect Does Surface Area Have on the Evaporation Rate of Water?

Category: **Chemistry—Physical Changes**
Project Idea by: **Ben and Hank Osborne**

Matter is anything that has **mass** (an amount of material) and **volume** (an amount of occupied space). The three common forms of matter on Earth, called the states of matter, are solid, liquid, and gas. A **solid** has a definite shape and volume; a **liquid** has a definite volume but no definite shape; a **gas** has no definite volume or shape.

Substances commonly exist in one of the three states, but they can be in any one of the three states depending on temperature. For example, water is commonly a liquid, but when cooled it forms a solid called ice. When liquid water is heated, it forms a gas.

The state of matter doesn't change the kind of particles of which a substance is made. Instead, the states of matter differ in how close their particles are as well as how tightly bonded the particles are. For example, each particle of liquid, gas, or solid water is made of one atom of oxygen combined with two atoms of hydrogen. Water particles in the gas state are far apart. Liquid water particles are closer together, and some are bonded to one another. Solid water particles, called ice, are close together and are the most tightly bonded.

When water changes from one state to another, there is a gain or loss of energy. States of matter in order from least to most energy are solid, liquid, gas. To change to a higher energy state, such as when water changes from ice (solid) to liquid or from a

SOLID +HEAT ⇌ LIQUID +HEAT ⇌ GAS
MELTING   VAPORIZING

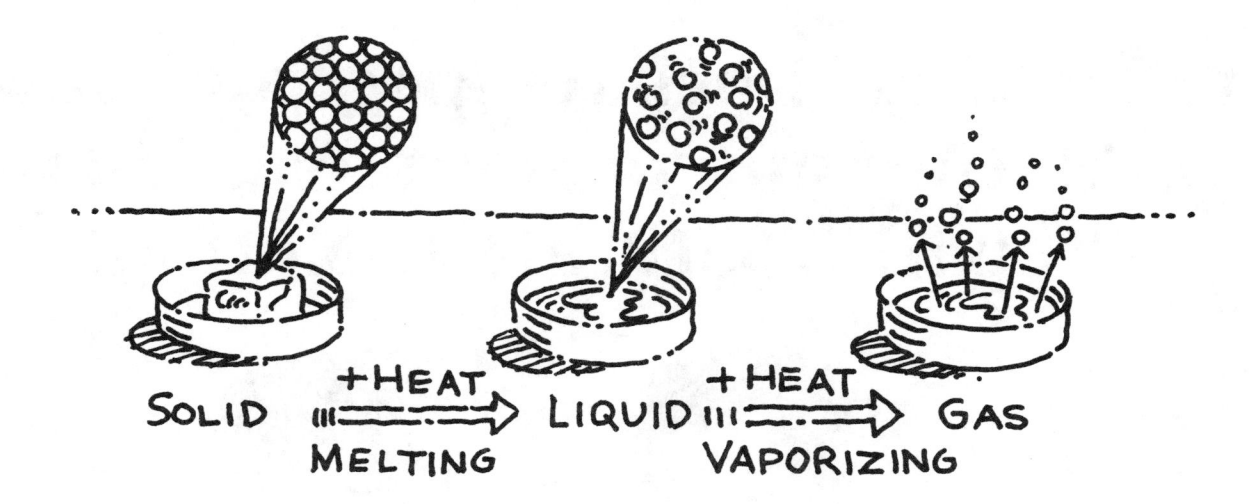

liquid to a gas, heat must be added. The process of changing from a solid to a liquid is called **melting**. The process of changing from a liquid to a gas is called vaporizing.

If vaporization happens at the surface of a liquid, the process is called **evaporation**. The gaseous state of a substance at a temperature at which that substance is usually in a solid or liquid state is called a **vapor**. When water evaporates, vapor is formed. **Evaporation rate** is the amount of liquid that evaporates in a certain amount of time. A project question might be, "What effect does surface area have on the evaporation rate of water?"

Clues for Your Investigation

Design a way to measure evaporation rate such as marking volume measurements on four or more containers with different-sized openings. For example, place a piece of tape down the side of each container. Then pour in a measured amount of water, such as 10 mL, and mark the water level on the tape. Continue adding the same amount of water in each container and marking its surface level on the tape until you have the amount of water in each container you need for your experiment. Place the containers next to each other. You can use the markings on the containers to measure the water lost to evaporation after a determined amount of time, such as one day. You may wish to mark the tape each day for one week.

Independent Variable: Surface area of a liquid

Dependent Variable: Evaporation rate

Controlled Variables: Temperature, amount of water at the beginning of the test, measuring period, method of measuring evaporation rate

Control: Container with the medium-sized opening

Other Questions to Explore

1. How does temperature affect the rate of evaporation?
2. What effect, if any, does the temperature of water have on the freezing rate?

Project 20

What Effect Does Temperature Have on the Amount of Solute Needed to Prepare a Saturated Solution?

Category: **Chemistry—Physical Changes**

Project Idea by: **Annie Frey**

A **solution** is a **homogeneous mixture** (a mixture that is the same throughout) of two or more substances. The two types of substances making up a solution are called a solute and a solvent. The substance being **dissolved** (separated into parts and spread throughout) is called the **solute**, and the substance doing the dissolving is called the **solvent**. A solution can exist in any state of matter. The substance present in the smaller amount is usually considered the solute. Solutions in which water is the solvent are called **aqueous solutions** and are the most common kind of solutions.

The strength of a solution is referred to as its **concentration** (the amount of solute in a specific amount of solvent). The more solute that is dissolved in a solvent, the greater the concentration of the solution. For example, in a glass of water, the more instant tea added to the water, the greater the concentration of tea in the solution. A glass of tea with a small amount of tea in it is said to be **dilute** (has a low concentration) in comparison to the more concentrated solution with more tea. If the solute has a color, the darker the color, the more concentrated the solution.

There is a limit to the amount of solute that will dissolve in a given amount of solvent. For example, when you add sugar to a glass of iced tea, it is a waste to keep adding the sugar once it starts settling to the bottom of the glass. No matter how much you stir, the extra sugar will not dissolve. When no more sugar will dissolve in the tea, a saturated solution is produced. A **saturated solution** is one in which the maximum amount of solute is dissolved in a solvent at a given **temperature** (a measure of how hot or cold a material is). When less than the maximum amount of solute is dissolved, the mixture is called an **unsaturated solution**. A project question might be, "What effect does temperature have on the amount of solute needed to prepare a saturated solution?"

Clues for Your Investigation

Use one solute, such as salt, sugar, or Epsom salts, and distilled water for the solvent. Keep the amount of water the same for each test. To vary the temperature, the water can be chilled in the refrigerator and warmed in the sun. CAUTION: Hot water from a faucet or prepared on the stove should be tested only with adult assistance. Do not prepare hot water in a microwave because it can get too hot and erupt when the solute is added.

For each test, add measured amounts of the solute to water. Add the solute a small amount at a time, stirring until the solute dissolves before adding more. When no more solute will dissolve and the solute begins to collect on the bottom of the container, record the amount of solute added as the amount needed to produce a saturated solution in the amount of water used. Compare the amounts of solute needed to make saturated solutions at different temperatures.

Independent Variable: Temperature of the solvent

Dependent Variable: Amount of solute

Controlled Variables: Type of solute, amount of water used, method of measuring solutes, method of stirring

Control: Water at room temperature

Other Questions to Explore

1. What effect does the type of solute have on preparing a saturated solution?
2. What is a supersaturated solution? What effect does the type of solute have on preparing a supersaturated solution?

Project 21

What Effect Does Surface Texture Have on Growing Crystals?

Category: **Chemistry—Physical Changes**

Project Idea by: **Sarah and Rachel Cathey**

A solid is the state of matter in which a substance has no tendency to flow under moderate pressure, resists forces that tend to deform it, and retains a definite size and shape. Simply stated, a solid has a definite shape and volume. Apples, books, rocks, and even your body are examples of solids.

Solids are very difficult to **compress** (squeeze together). This is because at the **microscopic level** (the level at which particles are so small that they cannot be seen except by magnification), the particles making up a solid are more closely packed together than liquids and gases. All particles vibrate (move back and forth), but those in solids do not move far from their places and cannot flow over or around one another. This results in solids having a definite shape and volume, and it is the reason that other matter cannot penetrate, or pass through, a solid. **Crystals** are solids with particles arranged in a regular, repeating pattern with flat surfaces. Most solids are **crystalline solids**, which are solids made of crystals. For example, when liquid water freezes, the water particles link together, forming ice crystals. A large piece of ice is made up of many small ice crystals that fit together like a puzzle. The shape of a crystal depends on the arrangement of the particles within it.

A **unit cell** is the smallest group of particles

within a crystal that retains the geometric shape of the crystal. For example, the unit cell of a table salt crystal is cubic. For salt crystals to form, the cubic cells must be able to move about so that they can be positioned with their **faces** (the flat surfaces of a solid) against one another, much like stacked boxes.

One way that crystals form is from a solute **precipitating** (separating) from a solution. Precipitation occurs when there is more solute than can dissolve in the solvent. As the water evaporates in an aqueous salt solution, the solution becomes more concentrated with salt; that is, as the amount of water decreases, there is more salt mixed with a smaller amount of water. When there is more salt than can dissolve in the remaining water, the salt precipitates. As the salt (solute) precipitates, its particles bond (link) together, forming unit cells that comprise a crystal. The more unit cells that bond together, the larger the crystal.

Crystals are found in many places, including inside rocks, on the ceiling and floors of caves, and in candy. Sugar crystals are grown on strings and sold as candy called rock candy. When a unit cell sticks to a surface and is stationary, it is more likely that other unit cells will bond to it. A project question might be, "What effect does surface texture have on growing crystals?"

Clues for Your Investigation

Decide on the type of crystal to grow, such as table salt, alum, or Epsom salts, as well as the procedure used for crystal growth. Grow the crystals from equal volumes of solution in identical containers. Place different surfaces in the solution such as a coiled wire and a coiled pipe cleaner. Determine how to measure the results; for example, at the end of a predetermined period of time, compare the amount of each test surface that is covered with crystals.

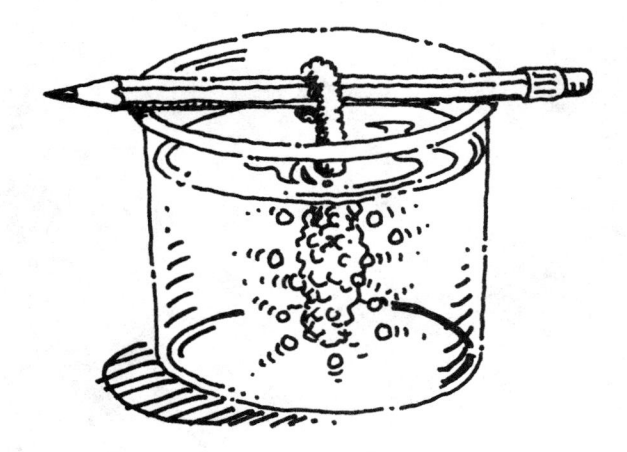

Independent Variable: Surface texture
Dependent Variable: Amount of surface covered with crystals
Controlled Variables: Type of solute; concentration of solute; amount of solution; type of container; temperature, humidity, light, and other environmental factors
Control: Container of solution with no hanging surfaces

Other Questions to Explore

1. What effect does the type of solute have on the shape of crystals formed from aqueous solutions?
2. What effect does temperature have on crystal growth?

Project 22

What Effect Does Temperature Have on the Thickness of Ketchup?

Category: **Chemistry—Physical Changes**
Project Idea by: **Lacey Russell**

Ketchup is an example of a heterogeneous mixture, which means that it is not the same throughout. Some of the particles in ketchup are dissolved and are spread throughout the mixture, but some particles remain suspended in the liquid.

Ketchup is a type of mixture called a **thixotropic liquid**, which increases in thickness when allowed to stand and decreases in thickness when shaken or stirred. This happens because when the substance is still, weak bonds form between the particles, linking them and forming a support frame. Since the support frame is weak, it is easily broken if the liquid is shaken, squeezed, or stirred; thus, the thickness decreases. But when the motion stops, the particles reconnect again, forming the support structure and thickening the mixture.

Toothpaste is another example of a thixotropic liquid. When left alone, it acts more like a solid. If you turn an open toothpaste tube upside down, the paste will not flow out. But if you squeeze the tube, the paste, even though thick, flows out much like a liquid would. A project question might be, "What effect does temperature have on the thickness of ketchup?"

HIGH ◄──── THICKNESS ────► LOW

Clues for Your Investigation

Design a way to test the thickness of different samples of ketchup at different temperatures. One way is to compare their thickness by measuring how easily they flow. You could place equal-sized blobs of ketchup at one end of a baking sheet. Then raise the end of the baking sheet with the ketchup samples to create an inclined surface. In advance, determine that one ketchup sample will be the control, such as the one at room temperature. Arbitrarily assign the control a thickness value of 5. Compare how fast the other samples of ketchup, which are at different temperatures, flow in comparison to the control. Rate each sample with a thickness number from 1 to 10, with 1 flowing the slowest and 10 the fastest. You may use fractions.

Independent Variable: Temperature
Dependent Variable: Flow rate
Controlled Variables: Thixotropic liquid (one brand of ketchup), measuring device for flow rate, measuring device for temperature, environmental factors
Control: Median temperature (room temperature can arbitrarily be used)

Other Questions to Explore

1. Would changing the concentration of the thixotropic liquid affect the results?
2. What is a dilatant and how is its thickness by temperature?

Project 23

What Effect Does the pH of Food Have on Preventing Tarnish on Copper Pots?

Category: **Chemistry—Chemical Changes**
Project Idea by: **Saba Javadi and Kate Foley**

A chemical is any substance with a definite composition made up of one or more elements (substances that contain only one kind of atom). **Compounds** are chemicals made up of two or more different elements. Examples of elements include the metal copper (Cu) and the gas oxygen (O), which is found in air. An example of a compound is a chemical made up of copper and oxygen: called copper oxide (CuO).

The formation of copper oxide involves a chemical change, which is the change of one or more substances to something new. Another name for a chemical change is a **chemical reaction**. Chemicals that are changed during chemical reactions are called **reactants**, and chemicals produced in chemical reactions are called **products**. If a chemical reaction involves the combination of oxygen with another element, the reaction is called **oxidation** and the product is called an oxide. In the formation of copper oxide, copper and oxygen are the reactants and copper oxide is the product.

The atoms on the surface of metals often combine with oxygen atoms from the air to form metal oxides. Copper surfaces, such as those on some cooking pots and coins, are often coated with different kinds of copper oxides. Any coating on a metal that discolors and/or dulls on the surface is called a

CHEMICAL REACTION

REACTANTS + → PRODUCT

COPPER (Cu) + OXYGEN (O) → COPPER OXIDE (CuO)

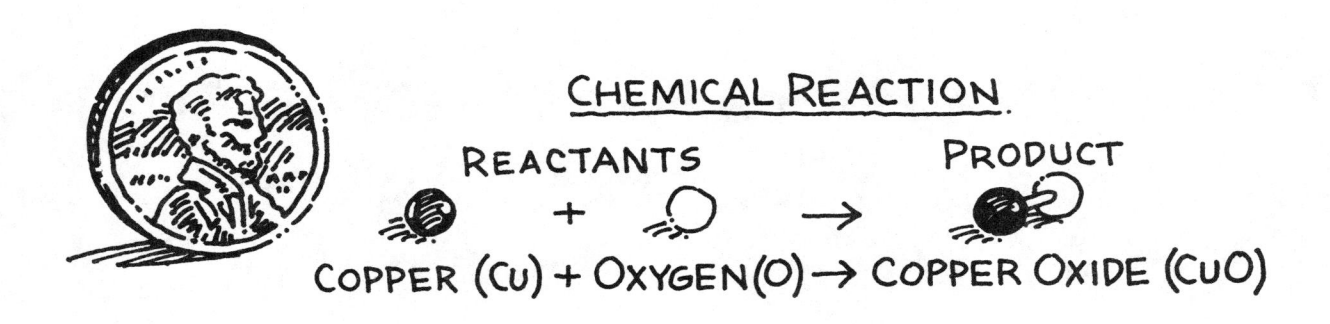

tarnish. The copper oxides on coins or other copper surfaces are considered a tarnish.

Tarnish is the result of a chemical change, and it can be removed by a chemical change such as occurs with an acid. An **acid** is a sour-tasting chemical that forms salt and water when mixed with a **base** (a bitter-tasting chemical, including metal oxides). Copper oxide can be chemically removed from a copper surface by soaking it in an acid such as vinegar or lemon juice. The special scale for measuring the strength of an acid or base is called the **pH scale**. The values on the pH scale range from 0 to 14. Water is **neutral** (neither an acid nor a base) and has a pH value of 7. Acids have a pH of less than 7, and bases have a pH greater than 7. The less the pH, the more concentrated the acid. The greater the pH, the more concentrated the base. A project question might be, "What effect does the pH of food have on preventing tarnish on copper pots?"

Clues for Your Investigation

Design a way to test the effect of acidic foods on the removal of tarnish from copper. One way is to use tarnished pennies and foods with different pH values. You do not have to know the exact value of the testing solution, just that the pH is different. For example, some vinegar has a pH of about 2.8 and distilled water is always 7. So vinegar and water can be mixed in different concentrations to produce solutions of different pH values. Tarnished pennies can be placed in the different acid solutions for a predetermined amount of time. Determine which solution cleans the coins faster. CAUTION: Even though vinegar is a food, it is an acid, so try not to get it on your skin. If you do get some on your skin, rinse it off thoroughly with water. While you perform the experiment, wear goggles to protect your eyes.

Independent Variable: pH of acid solution
Dependent Variable: Removal of tarnish from copper
Controlled Variables: Degree of tarnish on coins, number of coins for each test, temperature of solutions, time in testing solutions
Control: Water

Other Questions to Explore

1. Would other acidic foods work as well as the vinegar? (Citric acid is a weak acid found in citrus fruit such as lemon, lime, and grapefruit.)
2. What effect does temperature have on the speed of the reaction?

Project 24

What Effect Does the Concentration of a Mordant Have on the Colorfastness of a Natural Dye?

Category: **Chemistry—Chemical Changes**
Project Idea by: **Clay Hooper and Megan Witcher**

A dye is a substance used for changing the color of other things such as fabrics. Dyes contain a **colorant**, which is a substance that selectively absorbs and reflects visible light so that you see a certain color.

Visible light is light the human eye can see. White light is a combination of all light colors in the visible spectrum, which in order from least to most energy are red, yellow, orange, green, blue, indigo, and violet. When white light strikes cloth that is dyed red, the red colorant absorbs all of the colors in the light except red, which is reflected. This reflected light enters your eye, and you perceive the cloth as being red in color.

The colors in some dyed materials **fade** (become lighter in color) when exposed to sunlight or through washing. **Colorfastness** is a measure of how well a dyed material resists fading. A dyed material that resists fading is said to have greater colorfastness.

Colorfastness of a dye can be improved by using a substance called a mordant. A **mordant** is a chemical that bonds the colorant in a dye to a material. This happens because part of a mordant particle bonds to a particle in the material and another part of the mordant particle bonds to a dye molecule.

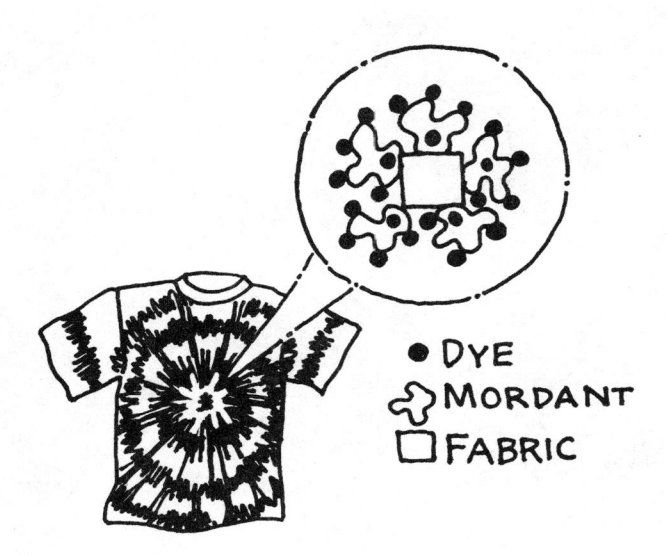

Mordants include alum, cream of tartar, and table salt. In some dyeing procedures, the material is soaked in a solution made by mixing a mordant with water, then the material is placed in a dye solution. A project question might be, "What effect does the concentration of a mordant have on the colorfastness of a natural dye?"

Clues for Your Investigation

Select a mordant and prepare four or more solutions with different concentrations of the mordant and distilled water. Place 4 or more pieces of white cotton fabric in each of the mordant solutions for a measured amount of time. Then place each piece of fabric in a selected dye, which might be a food dye such as blackberry juice or another dark-colored juice. For a control, place fabric that has not been treated with the mordant in the dye. Rinse the fabric in distilled water to remove excess dye. Dry, then test for colorfastness. For example, you might place the fabric pieces in sunlight for a measured amount of time. Whatever your method of testing colorfastness, keep one piece of fabric from each test out of the light for comparison in order to determine the degree of color change.

Independent Variable: Concentration of mordant

Dependent Variable: Colorfastness of dye measured by degree of fading

Controlled Variables: Type of dye and mordant, distilled water, color and type of fabric, time of soaking in the mordant and dye, temperature of soaking solutions, method of washing, time of fabric testing, method of measuring the degree of color of fabric

Control: Fabric not treated with mordant

Other Questions to Explore

1. Does the temperature of the mordant affect the colorfastness of the dye?
2. Does the type of mordant affect the colorfastness of the dye?
3. Is a mordant more effective if it is mixed with the dye?
4. Does the temperature of the dye affect colorfastness?
5. What effect does the concentration of the dye have on its colorfastness?

Project 25

How Effective Are Homemade Barometers in Predicting Weather?

Category: **Earth Science—Meteorology**
Project Idea by: **Emily Frazier**

The atmosphere is the blanket of gas surrounding a celestial body. **Atmospheric pressure** is the measure of the pressure that the atmosphere exerts on surfaces. Since Earth's atmosphere is composed of a mixture of gases commonly called **air**, atmospheric pressure is often called **air pressure**. Atmospheric pressure is measured with an instrument called a **barometer**; thus, atmospheric pressure is also called **barometric pressure**.

Changes in atmospheric pressure can be used to predict **weather** (the condition of the atmosphere). An increase in pressure is an indication of upcoming fair weather, and a decrease in pressure is an indication of upcoming stormy weather. A project question might be, "How effective are homemade barometers in predicting weather?"

Clues for Your Investigation

Design and construct a barometer. One type of homemade barometer can be made by covering the open end of a can with plastic wrap and securing it with a rubber band. Then glue the end of a 4-inch (10-cm) piece of straw to the center of the plastic. When the atmospheric pressure is high, it pushes against the plastic covering, causing it to curve into the can. This makes the free end of the straw point up. When the pressure is low, the plastic puffs up and the straw points down.

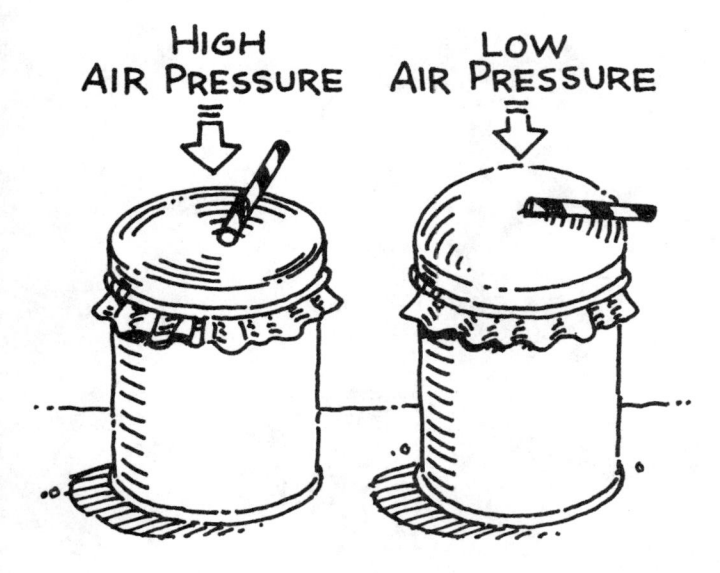

Use your homemade barometer to measure the atmospheric pressure at different times of the day each day for 1 or more weeks. Using the daily barometric measurements, predict upcoming weather. Record the prediction from national weather reported on TV, on the radio, or in a newspaper. Compare these predictions with the ones you make from your barometer measurements. Also record the actual weather for each predicted period.

Independent Variable: Barometric measurements
Dependent Variable: Weather predictions
Controlled Variables: Time of measurements, location of measurements
Control: Barometric measurements from TV, radio, or newspaper

Other Questions to Explore

1. How do atmospheric pressure changes affect cloud formation?
2. What effect do atmospheric pressure changes have on wind speed? Direction?

What Effect Does Humidity Have on Condensation Rate?

Category: **Earth Science—Meteorology**
Project Idea by: **Jared Cathey**

Temperature is a measure of how hot or cold a material is. The greater the temperature, the hotter the material. As the temperature increases, the motion of the particles in the material increase. As the temperature of a liquid increases, the speed of the liquid particles increases. As particle speed increases, the particles move farther and farther apart until finally they separate and are in a gas state. So an increase in temperature increases the evaporation rate of a liquid.

As the temperature of gas particles decreases, the speed of the particles decreases, causing **condensation** (the change from a gas to a liquid). The particles move closer together until they are in a liquid state. So a decrease in temperature increases the **condensation rate** of a gas, which is the amount of gas that condenses in a certain amount of time.

When warm, fast-moving particles of water vapor in the air collide with a cool surface, they lose some of their heat, which results in their moving at a slower speed. The cooler, slower-moving particles of gas form liquid water particles. For example, the cold outside surface of a soda can often has drops of water on it due to condensation of water vapor in the air.

On some days, the cold surfaces of cans or glasses are covered with more water than on other days. **Humidity** is the measure of the amount of water vapor in air. Does the amount of water that condenses on a surface depend on humidity? A project question might be, "What effect does humidity have on condensation rate?"

Clues for Your Investigation

Design a way to measure the rate of condensation on a material; for example, the time it takes for enough moisture to collect and form a drop that will roll down the side of a vertical surface. The experiment can be done on days of different humidity or in containers that have different humidities. A closed container with an open bowl of water in it will have a higher humidity than one without the water and an even higher humidity than one with a drying agent such as borax.

Dependent Variable: Humidity

Independent Variable: Rate of condensation

Controlled Variables: Testing containers, cooling procedure of containers, timing procedure

Control: Test with medium humidity (container without an open bowl of water or drying material in it)

Other Questions to Explore

1. What effect does the material on which water condenses have on the amount of condensation formed?
2. What effect does air temperature have on condensation?
3. What is dew point and how does it affect condensation rate?

Project 27

How Does Evaporation Affect the Salinity of Ocean Water?

Category: **Earth Science—Oceanography**
Project Idea by: **Donald Van Velzen**

Salinity is the salt concentration in a salt and water solution. The average salinity of seawater is 35 parts per thousand. This is written as 35 ppt, and it means that 35 parts of salt are in every 1,000 parts of seawater. While most samples of seawater have a salinity of 35 ppt, the salinity does vary from place to place. The salinity of seawater is usually between 32 ppt and 38 ppt.

Density is the ratio of mass to volume of a material. This property of matter allows you to compare materials of the same size and determine which is heavier.

Specific gravity is the ratio of the density of a material to the density of water. Specific gravity has no units. It compares the heaviness of a material to the same volume of water. No matter what units the densities are expressed in, specific gravity is the same. For example, mercury is 13.6 times as heavy as an equal volume of water. Thus, the specific gravity of mercury is 13.6. If the temperature is such that the density of water is 1 g/mL, the density of mercury would be 13.6 × 1 g/mL, or 13.6 g/mL.

Specific gravity can be used to determine the salinity of a liquid. Salt water has a greater density than fresh water, so it also has a higher specific gravity. The higher the salinity of an aqueous salt solution, the greater its specific gravity. A **hydrometer** is an instrument used to measure the specific gravity of a liquid. A hydrometer floats in a liquid. The higher it floats in the liquid, the greater the specific gravity of the liquid. A project question might be, "How does evaporation affect the salinity of ocean water?"

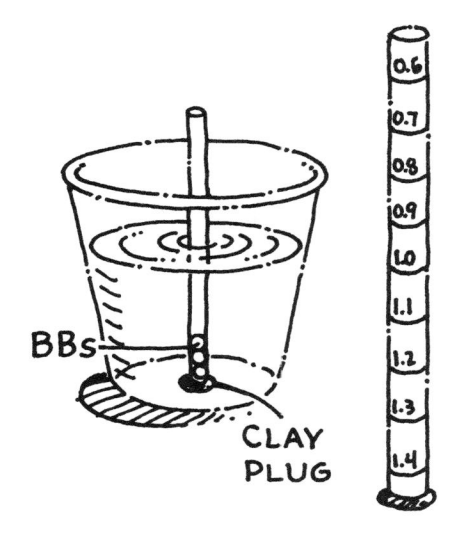

Clues for Your Investigation

Place a liquid made of a measured amount of salt and distilled water in an open container. Design a way to measure evaporation rate such as placing a strip of tape down the side of the container and marking the surface level of the water. At predetermined intervals, use a hydrometer to measure the specific gravity of the liquid. The hydrometer can be purchased or homemade. You can make your own hydrometer using a straw, BBs, and clay. In the figure, the scale printed on the straw shows the specific gravity higher and lower than the water, which is 1.0. The weight of the straw, the BBs, and the clay should make the hydrometer stand upright in fresh water, with 1.0 at water level.

Independent Variable: Evaporation rate
Dependent Variable: Salinity of water (determined by specific gravity)
Controlled Variables: Type of salt, distilled water, containers, amount of liquid, method of measuring, hydrometer, environmental conditions
Control: Specific gravity of distilled water

Other Questions to Explore

1. Does the type of solute affect the solution's specific gravity?
2. What effect does temperature have on specific gravity?

Project 28

What Effect Does the Type of Ground Cover Have on the Rate of Soil Erosion?

Category: **Earth Science—Physiography**
Project Idea by: **Alex and Drake Conner**

The physical nature of Earth's **crust** (the outer layer of Earth) is in a constant state of change. The changes are the result of **erosion**, the process by which rocks and other materials of Earth's crust are broken down and carried away. The part of erosion that involves only the breakdown of crustal materials is called **weathering**. Two weathering processes are mechanical weathering and chemical weathering.

Mechanical weathering is the breakdown of crustal material by physical means. Mechanical weathering is a physical change, meaning the appearance of a material changes, but its properties and makeup remain the same. For example, when a seed germinates in a crack in a rock, the growing plant that forms may push hard enough to split the rock. The rock has been physically changed in that it has been split into smaller pieces.

Chemical weathering is the breakdown of crustal materials due to chemical changes in the substances making up the crust. A chemical change produces one or more kinds of substances that are different from those present before the change. For example, iron in rocks combines with oxygen in the air, forming iron oxide (rust).

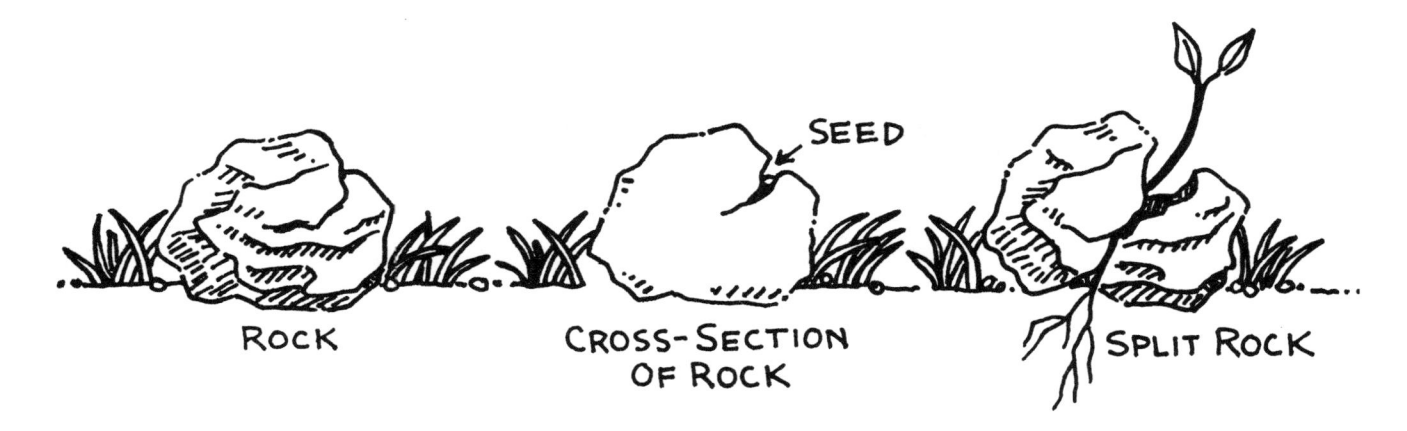

The moving part of erosion is caused by natural agents such as water and ice. For example, water in a river erodes a riverbank, forming both a solution and a suspension. When water in a river hits against the riverbank, material breaks away, and some dissolves in the water, forming a solution. Other materials that break away from the bank don't dissolve, but they mix with the water, forming a **suspension** (a liquid mixture made of parts that separate upon standing). The moving water carries the weathered materials away.

When new roads are built, material such as hay is often placed over the newly formed roadside to help prevent erosion. A project question might be, "What effect does the type of ground cover have on the rate of soil erosion?"

Clues for Your Investigation

Cover four or more equal-sized pieces of boards, with dirt. Cover the dirt with different types of material such as leaves, hay, and grass. Raise one end of each board the same amount so that it is at a slant to the ground. Design a way for equal amounts of water to rain down on the separate testing surfaces. One way to measure erosion is to collect and measure the amount of soil washed off the surface and collected at the lower end of each surface.

Independent Variable: Type of ground cover

Dependent Variable: Degree of erosion (measured by the amount of material washed away)

Controlled Variables: Size and slope of surfaces, type and amount of dirt, amount of water, type of watering method, measuring devices

Control: Soil without a covering

Other Questions to Explore

1. **What effect does the slope of the land have on the rate of soil erosion?**
2. **What effect does plant growth have on the rate of soil erosion?**

How Does the Texture of Paper Affect Its Printing Quality?

Category: **Engineering—Chemistry—Technology**

Project Idea by: **David VanCleave and Sebastian Mead**

Absorbency is the ability of a material to soak up a fluid such as water or ink. The absorption of liquid by paper is the result of the attraction between the liquid particles and the paper. The attraction between like particles is called **cohesion**, and the attraction between unlike particles is called **adhesion**. When the adhesion between the liquid particles and the paper is greater than the cohesion, the liquid is absorbed by the paper.

The degree of absorbency of paper affects the brightness and sharpness of any lines of the ink printed on it. Poor-quality ink prints are made on paper with low absorbency, partly because the ink that is not absorbed by the paper tends to smear and/or rub off the paper. Poor-quality ink prints are also made on paper with a very high degree of absorbency. This is because the paper absorbs so much ink that the ink shapes have blurred boundaries. The paper with just the right amount of absorbency produces ink prints with sharp, clear lines. **Texture** is how a surface feels, such as smooth or rough. A project question might be, "How does the texture of paper affect its printing quality?"

Clues for Your Investigation

Determine a way of measuring printing quality. One way is to stamp an ink print on papers with different textures. Using a magnifying lens, compare the sharpness of the borders of the print on each type of paper.

Dependent Variable: Texture of paper

Independent Variable: Quality of ink print

Controlled Variables: Shape of ink print, ink stamping procedure, measuring procedure, color of paper, weight of paper

Control: Medium-textured paper

Other Questions to Explore

1. Does the color of testing papers affect printing quality?
2. Does the weight of testing papers affect printing quality?
3. Copy paper has a suggested side for printing. Is the absorbency different for each side of the paper?
4. Does the print on newspaper and magazine pages affect absorbency rate?

What Type of Container Increases the Shelf Life of Bread?

Category: **Engineering—Food Technology**
Project Idea by: **Arielle Simner and Naomi Chalfin**

Shelf life is the period during which food may be stored and remain suitable and safe to eat. Two ways of identifying shelf life are date mark and expiration date. A **date mark** is a date stamped on the food package with instructions that read "use by [date]" or "best before [date]." A "use by" date appears on highly perishable food with short shelf lives such as milk and meats. These items may be dangerous to eat after the date. The "best before" date appears on foods with longer shelf lives such as breads and cookies. These foods are still edible after the date, but their taste quality may not be as good. For example, once the date on potato chips has passed, they will not be bad, just less crisp.

The **expiration date** on food tells you when you can expect the food to go bad. It doesn't mean that the food will be inedible on that date. Instead, it indicates when the food most likely will start to go bad. Whether a particular food has a longer or shorter shelf life than the expiration date or date mark depends on storing conditions. For example, if milk is left out of the refrigerator for a long time, the milk will probably spoil before its date mark.

The shelf life of food is affected by fat, moisture, oxygen, heat, and time. Foods with more fat spoil faster. Oxygen, moisture, and heat encourage the growth of microbes, which spoil food. So the longer foods are exposed to oxygen (a gas in air), moisture, and heat, the faster they spoil. The shelf life of foods increases if they are kept cool and away from sunlight. Thus, foods should be stored in dark, cool places.

The length of time bread can be stored before it becomes **stale** (a decrease in the quality of taste, due to age), **dehydrated** (dried out), or moldy is based on the type of bread and the storage conditions. Some bread is packaged in plastic and some in cellophane. Breads are also stored in different types of open and closed containers. A project question might be, "What type of container increases the shelf life of bread?"

Clues for Your Investigation

Use different kinds of bread containers including plastic bread sacks, cellophane bread wrappers, and a plastic box with a lid. The shelf life of bread is measured by the freshness of bread. One measure of freshness is its moisture content. Compare the time it takes for bread slices to dehydrate. Design a measuring scale to compare bread dryness. For example, the driest might be 1 and the most moist 10.

Independent Variable: Different types of bread containers

Dependent Variable: Time to reach dryness of 1 on your scale

Controlled Variables: Environmental conditions including temperature, light, and humidity, type of bread, size of samples, same "best before" date

Control: Bread without a container

Other Questions to Explore

1. How does temperature affect the drying of bread?
2. Staleness is a measure of the quality of a food's taste. How does temperature affect the staling rate of bread?
3. Mold is a sign of old or stale bread. How does water activity affect the growth of mold?

Project 31

How Does the Degree of Stretching Affect the Ability of Plastic Food Wraps to Keep Foods Fresh?

Category: **Engineering—Product Development**
Project Idea by: **Britney Fleming**

Diffusion is the movement of particles from one place to another. Particles diffuse from more **concentrated** (particles are grouped together) areas to areas of less concentration. One type of diffusion is the movement of particles through a permeable **membrane** (a thin sheet of flexible material). **Permeability** is the ability of a material to allow substances to diffuse through it.

Some membranes such as plastic food wrap are **semipermeable**, which means they have the ability to allow some particles to pass through but not others. A semipermeable material acts like a tea strainer—small particles pass through the holes, but large particles do not. The particles that diffuse through a permeable or semipermeable material move from the side of the material where they are at higher concentrations to the side where they are at lower concentrations.

The movement of the particles continues toward the side of low concentration until the concentrations on both sides of the membrane are equal. Once they pass through the membrane, the particles continue to randomly move until they are evenly spread out.

When the concentration of a certain type of particle is the same on both sides of the membrane, the particles continue to move through the membrane. But for every particle that moves through the membrane in one direction, a particle moves through the membrane in the opposite direction. Thus, the concentration on both sides of the membrane remains the same.

The plastic in food wraps and food bags is a semipermeable material. The more permeable the plastic, the greater the rate of diffusion of particles through the plastic; thus, the less effective the plastic is at keeping the food fresh. Plastic food wraps are stretched over food containers. A project question might be, "How does the degree of stretching affect the ability of plastic food wraps to keep foods fresh?"

Clues for Your Investigation

Design a way to stretch plastic food wraps. One way could be to pull the plastic with your hands. Stretch each piece with different amounts of force. Semipermeable plastic food wrap is permeable to iodine particles but not to starch particles. When iodine combines with starch, a blue-black substance is produced. To test the permeability of plastic wrap, determine the speed at which iodine diffuses through it. This can be done by placing a thick solution of starch and water in the center of a piece of plastic food wrap. Bring the sides of the wrap together and secure with a twist-tie, forming a closed testing bag. Make two labeled testing bags from each stretched plastic wrap being tested. Then place one bag of each type of plastic bag in a solution of iodine (tincture of iodine) and one of each type in water. Design a timing method. One way is to determine the time it takes for the first appearance of a blue-black color on the starch and water mixture, which happens when iodine particles come in contact with starch particles. In making the starch and iodine solutions, use distilled water. For the starch solution, add 1 teaspoon (5 mL) of cornstarch to every ¼ cup (63 mL) of water. The iodine solution can be made by adding 5 drops of tincture of iodine (found at the pharmacy) to ¼ cup (63 mL) of water. CAUTION: Iodine stains. It is also a poison, so heed the warnings on the bottle. Do not do this experiment if you are allergic to tincture of iodine.

Independent Variable: Degree of stretching of plastic wrap

Dependent Variable: Diffusion of iodine, measured by the appearance of the blue-black color

Controlled Variables: Concentration of iodine in iodine and water solution and amount of this solution used, concentration of starch in the starch and water mixture and amount used, container over which plastic is stretched, type of plastic wrap, distilled water, environmental conditions such as temperature and light

Control: Piece of plastic wrap that has not been stretched

Other Questions to Explore

1. How does temperature affect diffusion through plastic food wrap?
2. How does time affect diffusion through plastic food wrap?
3. How does the type of food wrap affect the rate of diffusion of particles?

Project 32

What Effect Does Triangle Size Have on the Strength of a Truss Bridge?

Category: **Engineering—Structural Engineering**

Project Idea by: **Rosemary Kalonaros and Megan Ganzenmuller**

In designing a bridge, an engineer must consider the types of forces that will be applied to the bridge. A **force** is a push or pull on an object. Two of the forces that must be considered when designing a bridge are gravity forces and lateral forces. **Weight** is the measure of **gravity**, which on Earth is a measure of the force pulling objects toward Earth's center. The weight or gravity of an object increases as the mass of the object increases.

Weight causes some structures to bend downward. When this happens, compression and tension are produced. **Compression** is a force that pushes materials together, and **tension** is a force that pulls materials apart. In the diagram, the weight of the bridge as well as the weight of the car causes the beam to bend. The top edge of the beam has shortened because the compression forces, indicated by the arrows pointing toward each other in the illustration, squeeze the materials together. The bottom edge of the beam has lengthened due to tension forces, indicated by the arrows pointing in opposite directions, stretching the material.

Lateral forces are those directed at the side of the bridge or other structure. These forces include those generated by things such as the wind, earthquakes, and explosions. As a **system** (different parts working together as one unit), a structure must be designed so that it can resist all forces to which it is subjected, including gravitational and lateral forces.

The most basic bridge design is a **beam bridge**. A log across a creek is one of the simplest beam bridges. Since beam bridges cannot span great distances, other types of bridges have been designed such as truss bridges. A **truss bridge** is a bridge with **trusses** (a simple skeletal structure made up of straight beams forming triangular shapes). A triangle is a geometric shape that has a small amount of flexibility. By using many combinations of triangles in a truss, the unit can be designed to carry a great deal of weight and span great distances. A project question might be, "What effect does triangle size have on the strength of a truss bridge?"

Clues for Your Investigation

Build small truss bridges with different-sized trusses and test their strength. The bridges can be built with simple materials such as craft sticks, toothpicks, and straws. The bridges must be of comparable length, width, and height, with trusses containing different-sized triangles. Design a way to test the strength of the bridges such as supporting the bridge ends and adding a measured amount of weight until each bridge breaks.

Independent Variable: Size of triangles
Dependent Variable: Strength of truss bridge
Controlled Variables: Type of building materials, type of strength-testing device, size of bridges
Control: Truss with the median size of triangles

Other Questions to Explore

1. **How do the vertical beams affect the strength of a truss bridge?**
2. **How does the strength of different truss designs, such as the Howe, the Pratt, and the Warren, compare?**

Project 33

How Steady Is the Moon's Angular Speed from One Day to the Next?

Category: **Mathematics—Angular Measurements**
Project Idea by: **Sarah Yount**

T he **apparent distance** between celestial bodies is how far apart they appear to be from an observer on Earth. This distance measured in degrees is called the **angular distance**.

The width and distance between your fingers can also be used to measure sky distances. Holding your hands at arm's length, use the diagram to measure different angular distances. A combination of measurements can be used such as measuring the distance between the stars of the Big Dipper as shown in the example.

The Moon, which is Earth's only natural satellite (a celestial body orbiting another), appears to be slower than some of the stars in moving across the night sky to the western horizon. The apparent race between the stars and the Moon is due to Earth's daily rotation on its axis, which causes celestial bodies to appear to move from east to west across the sky. Unlike the stars, which in relation to Earth are relatively stationary, the Moon revolves around Earth from west to east. It takes about 29 days for the Moon to complete its revolution. So each night the Moon appears to move toward the west because of Earth's rotation, but at the same time it is slightly moving toward the east because of its own revolution. It is sort of like watching people on a moving escalator. If one person slowly steps backward, it appears that everyone else is moving forward and passing the slower person.

Speed is a measurement of distance in a given time period. For example, a car traveling at 50 miles per hour moves a distance of 50 miles in a time period of 1 hour. The speed of celestial bodies is measured in degrees per a given time and is called **angular speed**. A project question might be, "How steady is the Moon's angular speed from one day to the next?"

Clues for Your Investigation

Measure the Moon's angular speed on several nights. Take measurements on clear, dark nights. Design a measurement method. One way is to use your hands to measure the distance between the Moon and a particular star. Record this distance as d_1. After 1 hour, again measure the distance between the Moon and the star. (Be sure it is the same star.) Record this distance as d_2. Make three more measurements, each 1 hour apart and all using the same star for reference. Record the distances as d_3, d_4, and d_5. Use the formulas in the table to determine the average angular distance and the angular speed of the Moon for that night. Compare this average to the average angular speed for other nights.

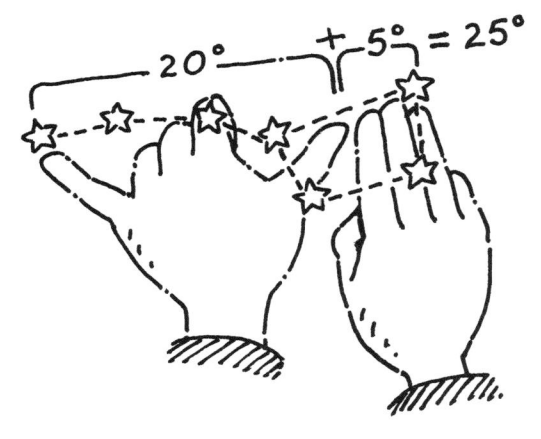

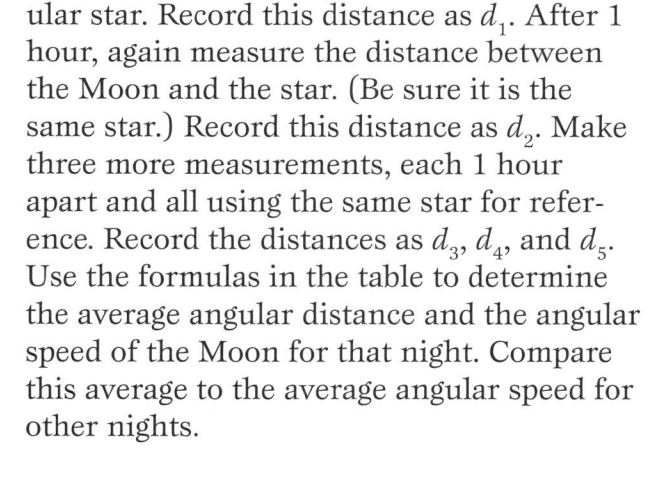

Time, t	Distance, D	Speed, D/t
1 hour	$D_1 = d_1 - d_2$	$S_1 = D/1$ hr
2 hours	$D_2 = d_1 - d_3$	$S_2 = D/2$ hr
3 hours	$D_3 = d_1 - d_4$	$S_3 = D/3$ hr
4 hours	$D_4 = d_1 - d_5$	$S_4 = D/4$ hr
Average	$D_{av} = (D_1 + D_2 + D_3 + D_4) \div 4$	$S_{av} = (S_1 + S_2 + S_3 + S_4) \div 4$

Independent Variable: Time
Dependent Variable: Angular distance over which the Moon moves
Controlled Variables: Measuring procedure, star used for comparison
Control: The Moon's average angular speed

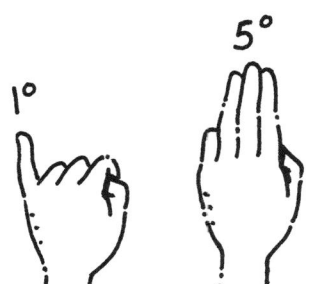

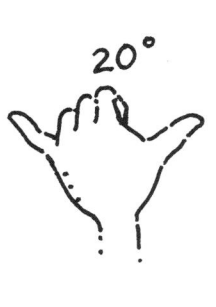

Other Questions to Explore

1. At what apparent angular speed do some of the more easily visible planets, such as Mars and Jupiter, move each day?
2. What is the apparent angular speed that stars move each day?

Project 34

How Does the Ratio of Two Dyes in a Mixture Affect Its Color?

Category: **Mathematics—Ratio**
Project Idea by: **Easton and Weston Walker**

A ratio is a pair of numbers used to compare quantities. It can be expressed in three different ways: (1) in words, (2) with a colon, or (3) as a fraction. For example, the mixture of three parts of blue paint with ten parts of yellow paint would look like this:

Comparison	In words using "to"	With a colon	As a fraction
Blue to yellow	3 to 10	3:10	3/10

A ratio is generally written as a simplified fraction. For the comparison of eyes to toes, you have two eyes and ten toes. The comparison of 2 to 10 would be simplified, so the ratio would be 1 to 5, 1:5, or 1/5. Order is important when writing a ratio. For the blue paint to yellow paint, the ratio is 3 to 10, not 10 to 3. Eyes to toes is 1 to 5, 5 to 1.

Paints, like other coloring materials, contain colorants. A colorant that dissolves in a liquid is called a dye. When dyes are mixed, a new color is produced. A project question might be, "How does the ratio of two dyes in a mixture affect its color?"

Clues for Your Investigation

Prepare two solutions using distilled water and two colors of food coloring. For example, if the dye colors to be used are blue and yellow, make testing solutions by mixing different ratios of blue and yellow. Make sure that each solution has the same amount of water. Design a method for mixing the dyes together in specific ratios such as by measuring out spoons of dye and pouring them into transparent cups. If the mixture is blue to yellow and the ratio is 1:2, then mix 1 spoon of blue dye and 2 spoons of yellow dye. Design a method of describing the color produced. One way is to compare the dyes with the color of the control, which is a 1:1 mixture. For example, a mixture of blue to yellow with a ratio of 1:1 is green. A mixture of blue to yellow with ratios of 2:1, 3:1, and 4:1 could be called light blue-green, medium blue-green, and dark blue-green, respectively.

Independent Variable: Ratio of dyes

Dependent Variable: Color of mixture

Controlled Variables: Measuring instrument, method of measuring color, dye solutions

Control: 1:1 dye ratio

Other Questions to Explore

1. What effect does the ratio of three or more dyes have on the resultant color of the mixture?
2. What effect does the ratio of dry colorants, such as colored sand, have on the resultant color of the mixture?

How Does a Refrigerant's Surface Area Affect How Well It Cools?

Category: **Physics–Energy—Heat**
Project Idea by: **Declan Morgan**

Temperature is the measure of how hot or cold a material is. Heat is the energy that flows from a warm material to a cool material. For a material's temperature to decrease, it must lose heat. For a material to increase in temperature, it must gain heat.

A **refrigerant** is a material used to cool other materials. Ice is a refrigerant that owes its effectiveness to the fact that it stays at its freezing temperature of 32°F (0°C) until it absorbs enough heat to melt.

Surface area is the size of the surface of an object. Surface area increases with the subdivision of the material. For example, crushing and grinding a solid will increase its surface area. A project question might be, "How does a refrigerant's surface area affect how well it cools?"

Clues for Your Investigation

Design a way to measure the effectiveness of a refrigerant such as ice. One way is to determine how fast ice cream melts when it's put in contact with ice having different surface areas such as different sizes of crushed ice and cubed ice. A measured amount of ice cream can be placed in a cup and surrounded by one form of ice. After a predetermined time, measure the amount of melted ice cream. To measure how much has melted, pour just the liquid into a measuring cup. Use the same amount of refrigerant for each test.

Independent Variable: Refrigerant's surface area

Dependent Variable: Effectiveness of refrigerant determined by amount of melted ice cream

Controlled Variables: Amount of ice cream, amount of refrigerant, containers, increments of time, measuring device

Control: Ice cream not surrounded by a refrigerant

Other Questions to Explore

1. How does insulating material affect a refrigerant's effectiveness?
2. How does the thermal conductivity of a material affect cooling or heating it?
3. Are gel ice packs better refrigerants than ice?

Project 36

What Effect Does Salt Concentration Have on the Specific Heat of an Aqueous Salt Solution?

Category: **Physics—Energy—Heat**

Project Idea by: **Daniel O'Leary and John Paul Carollo**

Heat is the energy that is transferred between objects because of differences in their temperature. It moves from an object with a higher temperature to one with a lower temperature. **Specific heat** is a measure of how well a material resists changing its temperature. A material with a low specific heat changes temperature easily; it has to gain or lose only a small amount of heat to increase or decrease its temperature. The opposite is true for a material with a high specific heat.

Pots and pans should be made with materials having low specific heats. That way, it doesn't take much heat to get the pot or pan hot, and most of the heat goes into cooking the food. Wood has a higher specific heat than metal. When the same amount of heat is added, a wooden handle on a pot does not get as hot as a metal handle.

Water has a very high specific heat: 1 cal/g °C. One calorie of heat is needed to raise the temperature of 1 gram of water 1°C.

This specific heat is for pure water. A project question might be, "What effect does salt concentration have on the specific heat of an aqueous salt solution?"

Clues for Your Investigation

Design a safe method of measuring temperature changes. One way is to cool the water and water-and-salt solutions instead of heating. Start with a measured amount of distilled water at room temperature. The water can be cooled by placing the container in the refrigerator or surrounding it with ice. Measure the temperature every 5 minutes for 30 or more minutes. Repeat the experiment using the same amount of water but with different amounts of salt mixed in.

Independent Variable: Amount of salt
Dependent Variable: Temperature change
Controlled Variables: Amount of water, type of containers, method of cooling, time intervals for measuring
Control: Distilled water

Other Questions to Explore

1. Do other kinds of solutes such as sugar or baking soda affect the specific heat of an aqueous solution?
2. How can the specific heat of different solids be compared?

Project 37

What Effect Does the Time of Day Have on Passive Solar Heating?

Category: **Physics—Energy—Solar**
Project Idea by: **Connor Fields**

Solar energy is a form of radiant energy from the Sun. Radiant energy is energy in the form of waves that can travel through space. **Solar heating** is a process of using solar energy to heat materials. There are two types of solar heating: active and passive. **Active solar heating** involves using special devices for absorbing and transporting solar energy. For example, some solar collectors are covered with tubes containing water. As sunlight strikes the collector, solar energy is absorbed and the heat is transferred to the water in the tubes. The hot water circulates through pipes to heat a building or to heat air blown into the building.

Passive solar heating does not use any mechanical means of distributing the collected heat; instead, it is direct heating from sunlight. For example, when sunlight comes through a window, it is absorbed by materials in the room, causing them to heat up. Heat is transferred from warm materials to cold materials until the temperature of the materials is the same. Thus, the heat transfer is by natural means. To get the most out of passive solar heating, buildings can be designed so that more sunlight will enter. In the Northern Hemisphere, the path of the Sun is from east to west across the southern sky. So a building with large windows facing the south will receive the greatest amount of sunlight.

Because of the variations in the amount of solar energy received during the day and at a particular location, generally neither active nor passive solar heating is the only heating source for a building. In order to know when solar heating is going to be the most effective, you must know when the greatest amount of solar energy can be collected during the day. A project question might be, "What effect does the time of day have on passive solar heating?"

Clues for Your Investigation

Design a way to measure the amount of solar energy at different times of day. One way is to design a solar cooker and determine how hot a container of water gets in the cooker in a given amount of time. Use a thermometer to measure the change in the temperature of the water. Repeat the procedure at different times during the day.

Independent Variable: Time of day

Dependent Variable: Amount of solar heat measured by water temperature

Controlled Variables: Solar cooker, amount of time the water is cooked, energy source (sunlight), measuring device (thermometer), environmental conditions such as humidity and cloudiness, position of cooker

Control: Median time

Other Questions to Explore

1. What effect does the color of the solar cooker have on the amount of solar energy absorbed?
2. How does the placement of the solar cooker in relation to sunlight affect the amount of solar energy absorbed?
3. What is a greenhouse, and how does the location of a greenhouse affect the amount of solar energy absorbed?

Project 38

How Does the Size of a Vibrating Surface Affect the Pitch of Its Sound?

Category: **Physics—Energy—Sound**
Project Idea by: **Zachary N.C. and Catherine E. Daunis**

Sound is energy produced by a vibrating material that can be heard and is also called **sound waves**, which are waves produced as a result of the vibration of a material. Vibration is a back and forth or up and down motion. Sound originates from a vibrating object that forces the particles of a **medium** (the material sound passes through) to vibrate. For example, if one end of a ruler is held securely to a table and the end extending past the table is pushed down, the free end of the ruler can be observed to vibrate (move back and forth) at a particular **frequency** (the number of vibrations per second). The vibrations of the ruler cause the air particles around the ruler to move back and forth at the same frequency, creating areas of **compression** (where the particles are pushed together) and **rarefaction** (where the particles are spread apart). Waves such as sound waves that have areas of compression and rarefaction are called **longitudinal waves**.

The movement of the air around the vibrating ruler transfers the sound energy through the air. The vibrating air enters your ears and hits against your eardrums causing them to vibrate. The frequency of the vibration of the eardrums is perceived by your brain as a specific sound called **pitch**. The

"How does the size of a vibrating surface affect the pitch of its sound?"

Clues for Your Investigation

Make one type of percussion instrument such as a drum in different sizes. Drums have plastic or other materials stretched tightly across a hollow plastic, wooden, or metal cylinder. Decide on the material to be used and make drums that have the same shape but vary in surface size. Decide on how the drums will be struck, and use the same procedure when testing each drum. Compare the pitch produced by each drum.

greater the frequency, the higher the pitch. As the length of the ruler decreases, its frequency increases, producing increasingly higher-pitched sounds.

Percussion instruments are musical instruments that make sound when you strike or shake them. Percussion instruments include drums, xylophones, gongs, and cymbals. Drums come in different sizes and shapes. A project question might be,

Independent Variable: Surface size of drum
Dependent Variable: Pitch
Controlled Variables: Material the drums are made of, shape of the drums, how the drums will be tested
Control: Medium-sized drum surface

Other Questions to Explore

1. What effect does the density of a vibrating material have on pitch?
2. What effect does the shape of a vibrating material have on pitch?

Project 39

How Does Density Affect the Buoyancy of Objects?

Category: **Physics—Mechanics—Buoyancy**

Project Idea by: **Amy Grabina and Britanny Manchio**

Buoyancy is the upward force of a fluid on an object placed in it. Archimedes (287–212 B.C.), a Greek mathematician, is given credit for explaining buoyancy. Floating is usually associated with water or air, but floating can describe any object that is suspended in any fluid, whether it is a liquid or a gas. The term **buoyant** is a measure of how well an object floats.

When an object such as a boat is placed in water, the submerged part of the object **displaces** (pushes aside) an amount of water whose weight is equal to the weight of the object. The heavier the object, the more water it displaces, and thus the lower it sits in the water.

An object floats or sinks in water because of the difference between the total downward force and the total upward force acting on the object. If no other forces are acting on the object, the downward force is equal to the weight (F_{wt}) of the object, and the upward force is equal to buoyancy (F_B). Weight is the measure of the force of gravity acting on the object. If the weight of the object is less than the buoyancy on the object, then the object floats. If the weight of the object is greater than the buoyancy on the object, then the object sinks. In diagram A, the weight of the boat is equal to the buoyancy on it, which is indicated by equal-length arrows; thus, $F_{wt} = F_B$, and the boat floats. In diagram B, the weight of the boat is greater than the buoyancy on it, which is indicated by unequal-length arrows; thus, $F_w > F_B$, and the boat sinks.

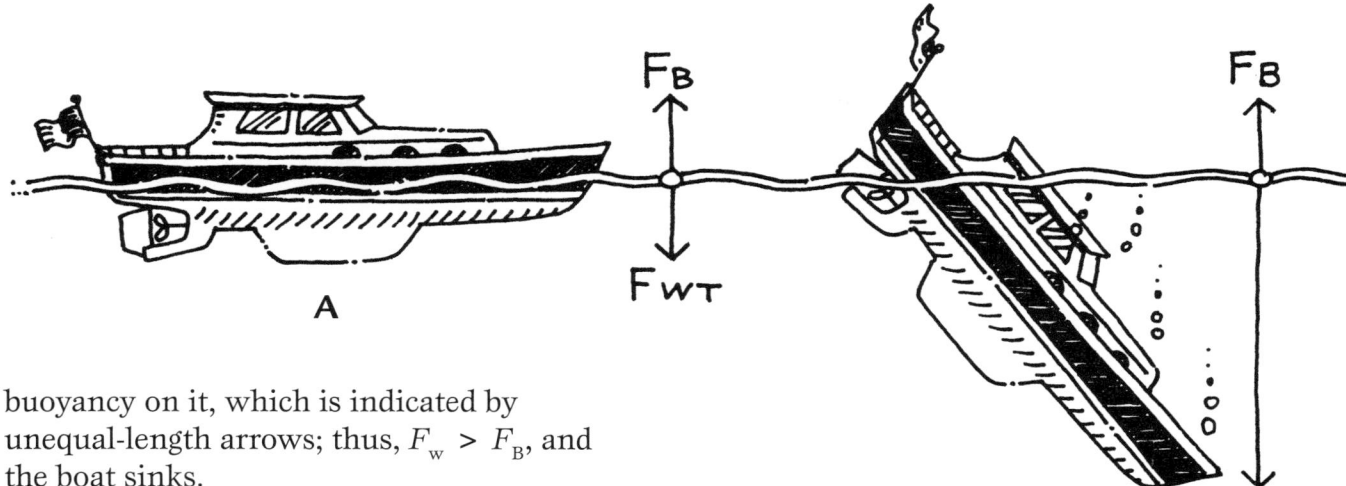

Since an object continues to sink into the water until it displaces an amount of water whose weight equals the weight of the object, would spreading out the weight make a difference in buoyancy? Volume is how much space an object takes up. For example, a piece of aluminum foil that is wadded into a tight ball has a small size and thus a small volume. If the same-size piece of aluminum foil has a boat shape, it has the same weight, but it now has a bigger size (a bigger volume).

Boats are made of different materials such as wood and steel. But boats are not solid pieces of material. Instead, boats have hollow spaces filled with air. Air is lighter than wood or metal. The more hollow spaces a boat has, the greater its volume. Since density is a measure of the mass of a given volume, a project question might be, "How does density affect the buoyancy of objects?"

Clues for Your Investigation

Build boats with the same mass but different volumes. Use the same kind and amount of material. Determine a way to measure the volume of each boat such as submerging the boats in water and measuring the amount of water displaced. With the mass and volume measurement, determine the density of each boat using this formula:

density = mass ÷ volume.

Determine a way to compare buoyancy such as by measuring the height of the boat above the waterline.

Independent Variable: Boats with different volumes

Dependent Variable: Buoyancy measured by the height of the boat above the waterline

Controlled Variables: Mass of the boats, material used, testing container for holding water, method of measuring buoyancy

Control: Median density

Other Questions to Explore

1. How does the placement of cargo in a boat affect its buoyancy?
2. What effect do building materials have on buoyancy?
3. What effect does salinity of ocean water have on buoyancy?

How Does Mass Affect the Period of a Pendulum?

Category: **Physics—Mechanics—Pendulum**
Project Idea by: **Chris Holifield**

A pendulum is a device with a **bob** (a weight) hung from a fixed **pivot** (the point on which something turns) so that it swings back and forth. When a pendulum hangs so that its bob is directly below the pivot, it experiences zero **net force** (the sum of all forces simultaneously acting on an object) and is said to be at its resting point. When the bob is pulled to one side and released, it repeatedly swings back and forth. One back-and-forth motion is called a vibration. The pendulum's **period (T)** is the time required to complete one vibration. The equation for period is:
period (T) = time/vibrations.

Displacement is the distance a pendulum moves to one side from its vertical position. Since the pendulum moves in an **arc** (a part of a circle), its displacement is an angular distance measured in degrees. The displacement angle is measured from the pendulum's vertical position. At a displacement angle of 15° or less, the periodic motion of the pendulum is the same; that is, regardless of the displacement of the pendulum, as long as it is 15° or less, the period of the pendulum will be the same.

Since weight is a measure of the gravitational pull on an object, would pendulums of different weights have different periods? As the mass of an object increases, its weight increases. A project problem might be, "How does mass affect the period of a pendulum?"

Clues for Your Investigation

Design pendulums that are the same except for the weight of the bob. They might be washers tied to a string. You can vary the weight of the bob by using a different number of washers for each pendulum. Pull the pendulums to one side so that they all start with the same displacement. Count the oscillations in a given time period.

Independent Variable: Weight of bobs
Dependent Variable: Period
Constant Variables: Length of pendulum, timing of period, displacement angle
Control: Median-weight pendulum

Other Questions to Explore

1. What effect does a displacement greater than 15% have on the period of a pendulum?
2. What effect does the stiffness of the bob support have on the period of a pendulum?
3. What effect does the size of the bob have on the period of a pendulum?
4. What effect does the length of a pendulum have on its period?

Appendix A

100 Project Ideas

Agriculture

1. What effect does the pH of soil have on plant growth?
   Independent variable: Soil pH
   Dependent variable: Plant growth

2. What effect does soil pH have on the color of flowers?
   Independent variable: Soil pH
   Dependent variable: Flower color

3. What effect does seed size have on the number of seeds that germinate?
   Independent variable: Seed size
   Dependent variable: Number of germinating seeds

4. How does the surface area of soil affect evaporation rate?
   Independent variable: Surface area
   Dependent variable: Evaporation rate

5. What effect does wind speed have on the evaporation rate of water from soil?
   Independent variable: Wind speed
   Dependent variable: Evaporation rate

Astronomy

6. How does the position of the Sun in the sky during the day affect the length of Sun shadows?
   Independent variable: Position of the Sun (determined by passing of time measured in minutes or hours)
   Dependent variable: Length of Sun shadows
   CAUTION: Do not look directly at the Sun because it can permanently damage your eyes.

7. How does the position of the Sun in the sky during the day affect the direction of Sun shadows?
   Independent variable: Position of the Sun (determined by passing of time measured in minutes or hours)
   Dependent variable: Direction of Sun shadows

8. How does the amount of light pollution affect the visibility of stars?
   Independent variable: Amount of light pollution (design a scale such as 1 is almost no light and 10 is the lights of a large city)
   Dependent variable: Degree of visibility

9. How does Earth's rotation affect the position of stars in a constellation in relation to one another?
   Independent variable: Earth's rotation (determined by passing of time measured in minutes or hours)
   Dependent variable: Star position

10. What effect does the color of a material have on it absorption of solar energy?
    Independent variable: Color of material
    Dependent variable: Absorption of solar energy (measured by an increase in temperature)

Biology

11. What effect does gender have on the rate of eye blinking?
    Independent variable: Gender
    Dependent variable: Rate of eye blinking

12. What effect does age have on the rate of eye blinking?
    Independent variable: Age
    Dependent variable: Rate of eye blinking

13. What effect does air temperature have on ant activity near an anthill entrance?
    Independent variable: Air temperature
    Dependent variable: Ant activity

14. How does the age of a plant leaf affect the leaf's size?
    Independent variable: Leaf age
    Dependent variable: Leaf size

15. How does the type of plant (monocot or dicot) affect the pattern of leaf veins?
    Independent variable: Plant type—monocot or dicot
    Dependent variable: Vein pattern in leaves

16. What effect does the location of water have on the direction of plant root growth?
    Independent variable: Location of water
    Dependent variable: Direction of plant root growth

17. What effect does the amount of sunlight have on the rate of chlorosis in grass?
    Independent variable: Amount of sunlight
    Dependent variable: Rate of chlorosis in grass

18. What effect does water pH have on the growth of the water plant elodea?
    Independent variable: Water pH
    Dependent variable: Growth of elodea

19. What effect does the amount of sunlight have on the growth of elodea?
    Independent variable: Amount of sunlight
    Dependent variable: Growth of elodea

20. How does temperature affect the blooming of a flower?
    Independent variable: Temperature
    Dependent variable: Flower blooming

21. How does the amount of light affect the blooming of a flower?
    Independent variable: Amount of light
    Dependent variable: Flower blooming

22. What effect does wind have on the rate of transpiration?
    Independent variable: Amount of wind
    Dependent variable: Rate of transpiration

23. What effect does cigarette tobacco in soil have on plant growth?
    Independent variable: Amount of cigarette tobacco in soil
    Dependent variable: Plant growth

24. Which paper found around the house has the fastest rate of biodegradability?
    Independent variable: Type of paper
    Dependent variable: Rate of biodegradability

25. What effect does the color of paper have on its rate of biodegradability?
    Independent variable: Color of paper
    Dependent variable: Rate of biodegradability

26. How does temperature affect the rate at which fruit ripens?
    Independent variable: Temperature
    Dependent variable: Rate of fruit ripening

27. How does light affect the rate at which fruit ripens?
    Independent variable: Light
    Dependent variable: Rate of fruit ripening

28. How does ethylene gas affect the rate at which fruit ripens?
    Independent variable: Ethylene gas
    Dependent variable: Rate of fruit ripening

29. What relationship is there between hair color and eye color?
    Independent variable: Hair color
    Dependent variable: Eye color

30. What relationship is there between hair color and skin freckles?
    Independent variable: Hair color
    Dependent variable: Skin freckles

31. How similar are the fingerprints of siblings?
    Independent variable: Siblings
    Dependent variable: Fingerprints

32. What effect does the period of time an eye is closed have on its pupil size?
    Independent variable: Time eye is closed
    Dependent variable: Pupil size

33. How does temperature affect the rate of insect metamorphosis?
    Independent variable: Temperature
    Dependent variable: Rate of metamorphosis

34. What effect does gender have on the sense of smell?
    Independent variable: Gender
    Dependent variable: Sense of smell

35. What effect does age have on the sense of smell?
    Independent variable: Age
    Dependent variable: Sense of smell

36. What effect does age have on the sense of touch?
    Independent variable: Age
    Dependent variable: Sense of touch

37. What effect does gender have on the sense of touch?
    Independent variable: Gender
    Dependent variable: Sense of touch

Chemistry

38. What effect does the type of solute have on the rate of crystallization?
    Independent variable: Type of solute
    Dependent variable: Rate of crystallization

39. What effect does the temperature of a solution have on the rate of crystallization?
    Independent variable: Temperature of a solution
    Dependent variable: Rate of crystallization

40. During crystallization, what effect does the rate of evaporation have on the size of crystals formed?
    Independent variable: Rate of evaporation
    Dependent variable: Crystal size

41. How does the pH of water affect the rate of the rusting of iron?
    Independent variable: Water pH
    Dependent variable: Rate of rusting

42. What effect does exercise have on the production of carbon dioxide in humans?
    Independent variable: Exercise
    Dependent variable: Carbon dioxide production

43. What is the effect of salt on the freezing point of water?
    Independent variable: Amount of salt
    Dependent variable: Freezing point of water
44. What effect does the type of solute have on degree of solubility?
    Independent variable: Type of solute
    Dependent variable: Degree of solubility (measured by the amount of solute that can be dissolved in a specific amount of solvent)

Earth Science

45. What effect does the amount of ground cover have on soil concentration in runoff?
    Independent variable: Amount of ground cover
    Dependent variable: Soil concentration in runoff
46. What effect does the type of ground cover have on soil concentration in runoff?
    Independent variable: Type of ground cover
    Dependent variable: Soil concentration in runoff
47. What effect does plant density have on soil erosion?
    Independent variable: Plant density
    Dependent variable: Soil erosion
48. What effect do the type of plant roots have on soil erosion?
    Independent variable: Type of plant roots
    Dependent variable: Soil erosion
49. How does the mixture of mineral solutions affect crystal growth?
    Independent variable: Mixture of solutions
    Dependent variable: Crystal growth
50. How does soil color affect the cooling of land?
    Independent variable: Soil color
    Dependent variable: Temperature change of the soil
51. What effect does the Sun's sky position have on air temperature?
    Independent variable: Sun's sky position (determined by time measured in hours)
    Dependent variable: Air temperature
52. How does the difference between land and water temperature affect the direction of wind?
    Independent variable: Temperature difference between land and water
    Dependent variable: Wind direction
53. How does the depth of water affect the altitude of water waves?
    Independent variable: Depth of water
    Dependent variable: Altitude of water waves
54. How does wind direction affect direction of surface currents?
    Independent variable: Wind direction
    Dependent variable: Current direction
55. What effect does the concentration of dust particles have on sky color?
    Independent variable: Dust particle concentration
    Dependent variable: Sky color
56. What effect does dust particle size have on sky color?
    Independent variable: Dust particle size
    Dependent variable: Sky color
57. How does air pressure affect the type of clouds formed?
    Independent variable: Air pressure
    Dependent variable: Cloud type
58. How does air temperature affect the type of clouds formed?
    Independent variable: Air temperature
    Dependent variable: Cloud type
59. What effect does wind speed have on the type of clouds formed?
    Independent variable: Wind speed
    Dependent variable: Cloud type

Engineering

60. What effect does the shape of an object have on its strength?
    Independent variable: Shape of object
    Dependent variable: Strength
61. Which brand of antacid tablet is the best at neutralizing stomach acid?
    Independent variable: Brand of antacid tablet
    Dependent variable: Degree of neutralization
62. Which brand of hair spray holds hair in place the longest time?
    Independent variable: Brand of hair spray
    Dependent variable: Holding time
63. Which brand of toilet paper decomposes the fastest in water?
    Independent variable: Brand of toilet paper
    Dependent variable: Rate of decomposition
64. Which brand of detergent has the most effect on stain removal from clothes?
    Independent variable: Brand of detergent
    Dependent variable: Degree of stain removal
65. Which type of cloth is the most resistant to food stain?
    Independent variable: Type of cloth
    Dependent variable: Degree of resistance to food stain

66. Which brand of shampoo produces the most lather?
    Independent variable: Brand of shampoo
    Dependent variable: Amount of lather

67. What effect does borax concentration have on softening water?
    Independent variable: Borax concentration
    Dependent variable: Degree of water softness

68. Which brand of washable colored markers does water most effectively remove from skin?
    Independent variable: Brand of washable colored markers
    Dependent variable: Degree of water solubility

Mathematics

69. How does age affect the mean height of a group?
    Independent variable: Age
    Dependent variable: Height

70. How does gender affect the mean height of a group?
    Independent variable: Gender
    Dependent variable: Height

71. How does the height of a rain gauge affect the distance between scale measurements?
    Independent variable: Height of rain gauge
    Dependent variable: Distance between scale measurements

72. How does the diameter of a rain gauge affect the distance between scale measurements?
    Independent variable: Diameter of rain gauge
    Dependent variable: Distance between scale measurements

Physics

73. How does the length of the string of a stringed instrument affect pitch?
    Independent variable: String length
    Dependent variable: Pitch

74. How does the thickness of the string of a stringed instrument affect pitch?
    Independent variable: String thickness
    Dependent variable: Pitch

75. How does the volume of water in a glass bottle affect the pitch of the sound produced when the bottle is struck?
    Independent variable: Volume of water
    Dependent variable: Pitch

76. How does the volume of water in a glass bottle affect the pitch of the sound produced when air is blown across the mouth of the bottle?
    Independent variable: Volume of water
    Dependent variable: Pitch

77. How do the number of coils in a solenoid affect the strength of an electromagnet?
    Independent variable: Number of coils in a solenoid
    Dependent variable: Magnetic strength

78. What effect does the intermittent use of a dry-cell battery have on its life?
    Independent variable: Time intervals of use of a dry-cell battery
    Dependent variable: Length of life of a dry-cell battery

79. What effect does the type of material charged have on the time it holds a static charge?
    Independent variable: Type of material
    Dependent variable: Time of holding a static charge

80. What effect does humidity have on the strength of a static charge?
    Independent variable: Humidity
    Dependent variable: Strength of a static charge

81. What effect does temperature have on the strength of a static charge?
    Independent variable: Temperature
    Dependent variable: Strength of a static charge

82. Which brand of battery lasts the longest?
    Independent variable: Brand of battery
    Dependent variable: Time to discharge the battery

83. What effect does the wattage of a lightbulb have on the amount of light it emits?
    Independent variable: Wattage of lightbulb
    Dependent variable: Amount of light

84. What effect does the number of strokes of a magnet on a nail have on the degree the nail is magnetized?
    Independent variable: Strokes of a magnet on a nail
    Dependent variable: Degree of magnetism

85. How does the position of the fulcrum in a first-class lever affect the weight it can lift?
    Independent variable: Fulcrum position
    Dependent variable: Weight lifted

86. How does the position of the fulcrum in a first-class lever affect the force needed to lift an object?
    Independent variable: Fulcrum position
    Dependent variable: Force applied

87. What effect does temperature have on the elasticity of a rubber ball?
    Independent variable: Temperature
    Dependent variable: Elasticity of a rubber ball (measured by the height the dropped ball bounces)

88. What effect does the amount of a lubricant have on friction between a marble rolling down a wooden incline?
    Independent variable: Amount of lubricant
    Dependent variable: Amount of friction

89. What effect does the temperature of a lubricant have on friction between a marble rolling down an incline?
    Independent variable: Temperature of lubricant
    Dependent variable: Amount of friction

90. What effect does the diameter of a string have on its strength?
    Independent variable: String diameter
    Dependent variable: Strength (measured by supporting weight)

91. What effect does the number of fibers in a string have on its strength?
    Independent variable: Number of fibers
    Dependent variable: Strength (measured by supporting weight)

92. What effect does the thickness of plastic have on the weight it will hold?
    Independent variable: Thickness of plastic
    Dependent variable: Weight supported

93. How does wing shape affect flight distance of a glider?
    Independent variable: Wing shape
    Dependent variable: Flight distance

94. What effect does the viscosity of a fluid material have on the buoyancy of an object in it?
    Independent variable: Fluid viscosity
    Dependent variable: Object buoyancy

95. What effect does the density of an object have on its buoyancy in water?
    Independent variable: Object density
    Dependent variable: Object buoyancy in water

96. In what type of light is fluorescent ink most effective?
    Independent variable: Type of light
    Dependent variable: Effectiveness of fluorescent ink (measured by brightness)

97. What effect does the size of a prism have on the spectrum produced?
    Independent variable: Prism size
    Dependent variable: Spectrum

98. What effect does the type of metal have on conducting heat?
    Independent variable: Type of metal
    Dependent variable: Rate of heat conduction

99. What effect does paint color have on its colorfastness when exposed to solar energy?
    Independent variable: Paint color
    Dependent variable: Degree of fading in sunlight

100. What effect does the mass of an object have on momentum?
    Independent variable: Mass of object
    Dependent variable: Momentum

Appendix B

Science Project and Reference Books

SCIENCE PROJECT BOOKS

Bochinski, Julianne Blair. *The Complete Handbook of Science Fair Projects.* Hoboken, NJ: Wiley, 2004.

Bonnet, Robert L., and G. Daniel Keen. *Botany: 49 Science Fair Projects.* Blue Ridge Summit, PA.: Tab Books, 1989.

———. *Botany: 49 More Science Fair Projects.* Blue Ridge Summit, PA: Tab Books, 1991.

Cobb, Vicki. *How to Really Fool Yourself.* New York: Wiley, 1999.

———. *Science Experiments You Can Eat.* New York: Harper & Row, 1994.

———. *See for Yourself: More Than 100 Experiments for Science Fairs and Projects.* New York: Scholastic, 2001.

DiSpezic, Michael. *Super Sensational Science Fair Projects.* New York: Sterling Publishing Co., Inc., 2001.

Hershey, David R. *Plant Biology Science Projects.* New York: Wiley, 1995.

Hilleman, Anne, and Mina Yamashita. *Done in the Sun: Solar Projects for Children.* Sante Fe, NM: SunstonePress, 1983.

Levaren, Maxine. *Science Fair Projects for Dummies.* Hoboken, NJ: Wiley, 2003.

O'Leary, Nancy K., and Susan Shelly. *The Complete Idiot's Guide to Science Fair Projects.* New York: Alpha Books, 2003.

Marks, Diana F. *Glues, Brews, and Goos: Recipes and Formulas for Almost Any Classroom Project.* Englewood, CO: Teacher Ideas Press, 1996.

Rosner, Marc. *Great Science Fair Projects.* New York: Wiley, 2000.

VanCleave, Janice. *Janice VanCleave's A + Projects in Astronomy.* Hoboken, NJ: Wiley, 2002.

———. *Janice VanCleave's A + Projects in Biology.* New York: Wiley, 1993.

———. *Janice VanCleave's A + Projects in Chemistry.* New York: Wiley, 1993.

———. *Janice VanCleave's A + Projects in Earth Science.* New York: Wiley, 1999.

———. *Janice VanCleave's A + Projects in Physics.* Hoboken, NJ: Wiley, 2003.

———. *Janice VanCleave's Guide to the Best Science Fair Projects.* New York: Wiley, 1997.

———. *Janice VanCleave's Guide to More of the Best Science Fair Projects.* New York: Wiley, 2000.

———. *Janice VanCleave's Help! My Science Project Is Due Tomorrow!* New York: Wiley, 2002.

———. *Janice VanCleave's Plants.* New York: Wiley, 1997.

———. *Janice VanCleave's Solar System.* New York: Wiley, 2000.

Vecchione, Glen. *100 Amazing Make-It-Yourself Science Fair Projects.* New York: Sterling Publishing Co., Inc., 1998.

———. *100 First-Prize Make-It-Yourself Science Fair Projects.* New York: Sterling Publishing Co., Inc., 1998.

Wood, Robert W. *Science for Kids: 39 Easy Astronomy Experiments.* Blue Ridge Summit, PA., 1991.

REFERENCE BOOKS

Agriculture

Bial, Raymond. *A Handful of Dirt.* New York: Walker and Company, 2000.

Ellis, Barbara, and Fern Marshall Bradley. *The Organic Gardener's Handbook of Natural Insects & Disease Control.* Emmaus, PA: Rodale Press, 1996.

Fedor, John. *Organic Gardening.* Pleasantville, NY: Readers Digest, 2001.

Ford, Peter. *Home Farm Handbook.* Hauppauge, NY: Barron's 2000.

Frederic, Katie. *Guide to Growing Healthy Houseplants.* Des Moines, IA: Meredith Books, 2005.

Hamilton, Geoff. *Organic Gardening.* New York: DK Publishing, 2004.

Hart, Avery, and Paul Mantell. *Kids Garden.* Charlotte, VT: Williamson Publishing Co., 1995.

Hessayon, D. G. *The House Plant Expert.* New York: Sterling Publishing Co., 2003.

Hodgson, Larry. *Houseplants for Dummies.* New York: Wiley, 1998.

Lovejoy, Sharon. *Trowel & Error.* New York: Workman Publishing, 2003.

MacCaskey, Michael, and Bill Marker. *Gardening for Dummies.* New York: Wiley, 1999.

Marker, Bill. *Container Gardening for Dummies.* New York: Wiley, 1998.

Roberts, Juliet. *Organic Kitchen Garden.* London: Coran Octopus Limited, 2005.

Roth, Sally, and Pamela K. Peirce. *All About Container Gardening.* Des Moines, IA: Meredith Books, 2001.

Speichert, Greg, and Sue Speichert. *All About Water Gardening.* Des Moines, IA: Meredith Books, 2001.

Astronomy

Asimov, Isaac. *Astronomy Projects.* Milwaukee: Gareth Stevens Publishing, 1996.

Couper, Heather, and Nigel Henbest. *How the Universe Works.* Pleasantville, NY: The Reader's Digest Association, Inc., 1994.

De Pree, Christopher. *The Complete Idiot's Guide to Astronomy.* New York: Alpha Books, 1999.

Dowswell, Paul. *First Encyclopedia of Space.* London: Usborne, 2001.

Farndon, John. *1000 Facts on Space.* New York: Barnes and Noble, 2005.

Filkin, David. *Stephen Hawking's Universe.* New York: Basic Books, 1997.

Maran, Stephen P. *Astronomy for Dummies.* Hoboken, NJ: Wiley, 2005.

Mechler, Gary. *Night Sky.* New York: Scholastic, 1999.

Mitton, Simon, and Jacqueline Mitton. *Astronomy.* Oxford, New York: Oxford University Press, 1995.

———. *The Scholastic Encyclopedia of Space.* New York: Scholastic, 1998.

Morgan, Ben. *Star Gazer.* London: DK Publisher, 2005.

Pasachoff, Jay M. *Peterson First Guides: Astronomy.* New York: Houghton Mifflin, 1988.

Rey, H. A. *The Stars.* Boston: Houghton Mifflin, 1976.

Richard, Paul. *A Handbook to the Universe.* Chicago: Chicago Review Press, 1993.

Ride, Sally, and Tom O'Shaughnessy. *Exploring Our Solar System.* New York: Random House, 2003.

Ridpath, Ian. *Stars and Planets Atlas.* New York: Facts on File, Inc., 1997.

Scott, Carile. *Stars and Planets.* Boston: Houghton Mifflin, 2005.

Slavin, Bill. *The Planets.* Toronto, ON: Kids Can Press, 1998.

Steele, Philip. *Black Holes and Other Space Phenomena.* New York: Kingfisher, 1995.

Walker, Jane. *The Solar System.* Brookfield, CT: The Millbrook Press, 1994.

Zim, Herbert S. *Stars.* New York: Golden Press, 1985.

Biology

Barnes, Kate, and Steve Weston. *The Human Body.* New York: Barnes and Noble, 1997.

Beckelman, Laurie. *The Human Body.* Pleasantville, NY: Reader's Digest, 1999.

Bender, Lionel. *Human Body.* New York: Crescent Books, 1992.

Berger, Melvin. *Scholastic Science Dictionary.* New York: Scholastic, 2000.

Burnie, David. *Nature Activities: Bug Hunters.* London: Dorling Kindersley, 2005.

Cash, Terry, Steve Parker, and Barbara Taylor. *175 More Science Experiments.* New York: Random House, 1991.

Clark, John O. E. *A Visual Guide to the Human Body.* New York: Barnes and Noble, 1999.

D'Amico, Joan, and Karen Eich Drimmond. *The Science Chef.* New York: Wiley, 1995.

Dispezio, Michael A. *Optical Illusion Magic.* New York: Sterling Publishing Co., Inc., 2002.

Farndon, John. *1000 Facts on Animals.* New York: Barnes and Noble, 2004.

———. *1000 Facts on Human Body.* New York: Barnes and Noble, 2002.

Gibson, Gary. *Science for Fun Experiments.* Brookfield, CT: Copper Beech Books, 1996.

Grassy, John, and Chuck Keene. *Mammals.* New York: Scholastic, 2005.

Kalumuck, Karen E. *Human Body Explorations.* Dubuque, IA: Kendall/Hung Publishing Company, 2000.

Kapit, Wynn, and Lawrence M. Elson. *The Anatomy Coloring Book.* New York: HarperCollins, 2001.

NatureScope: Trees Are Terrific! Washington, DC: National Wildlife Federation, 1992.

Parker, Steve. *How the Body Works.* Pleasantville, NY: Reader's Digest, 1994.

———. *The Human Body.* Brookfield, CT: Copper Beech Books, 1995.

———. *Touch, Taste and Smell.* New York: Franklin Watts, 1982.

Pascoe, Elaine, and Nicole Bowman. *Seeds and Seedlings.* Woodbridge, CT: Blackbirch Press, 1996.

Seelig, Tina L. *Incredible Edible Science.* New York: W. H. Freeman, 1994.

Seymour, Simon. *Science Dictionary.* New York: HarperCollins, 1994.

Siegfried, Donna. *Biology for Dummies.* Hoboken, NJ: Wiley, 2005.

Stein, Sara. *The Body Book.* New York: Workman Publishing, 1992.

Twist, Clint. *1000 Facts on Oceans.* New York: Barnes and Noble, 2005.

Unwin, Mike, and Helen Edom. *Science with Plants*. London: Usborne Books, 1993.
VanCleave, Janice. *Janice VanCleave's Biology for Every Kid*. New York: Wiley, 1990.
———. *Janice VanCleave's Food and Nutrition for Every Kid*. New York: Wiley, 1990.
———. *Janice VanCleave's Insects*. New York: Wiley, 1998.
———. *Janice VanCleave's The Human Body for Every Kid*. New York: Wiley, 1995.
Walker, Richard. *The Children's Atlas of the Human Body*. Brookfield, CT: Millbrook Press, 1994.
Walpole, Brenda. *Pocket Book of the Human Body*. New York: Simon & Schuster, 1987.
Weiner, Esther. *The Incredible Human Body*. New York: Scholastic, 1996.
Weise, Jim. *Head to Toe Science*. New York: Wiley, 2000.

Chemistry

Branzei, Sylvia. *Grossology*. Reading, MA: Addison-Wesley, 1995.
Edom, Helen. *Science with Water*. London: Usborne, 1992.
Epp, Dianne N. *The Chemistry of Food Dyes*. Middletown, OH: Terrific Science Press, 1995.
———. *The Chemistry of Natural Dyes*. Middletown, OH: Terrific Science Press, 1995.
Headlam, Catherine. *The Kingfisher Science Encyclopedia*. New York: Kingfisher Books, 1991.
Heiserman, David L. *Exploring Chemical Elements and Their Compounds*. Blue Ridge Summit, PA: Tab Books, 1992.
Kenda, Margaret, and Phyllis S. Williams. *Science Wizardry for Kids*. Hauppauge, NY: Barron's 1992.
Levine, Shar, and Allison Grafton. *Einstein's Science Parties: Easy Parties for Curious Kids*. New York: Wiley, 1994.
Moore, John T. *Chemistry for Dummies*. Hoboken, NJ: Wiley, 2003.
Strauss, Michael. *Where Puddles Go*. Portsmouth, NH: Heinemann, 1995.
VanCleave, Janice. *Chemistry for Every Kid*. New York: Wiley, 1989.
Wellnitz, William R. *Homemade Slime & Rubber Bones!* Blue Ridge Summit, PA.: Tab Books, 1993.

Earth Science

Allaby, Michael. *How the Weather Works*. New York: Reader's Digest, 1995.
Brewer, Duncan. *1000 Facts on Mammals*. New York: Barnes and Noble, 2002.
Burroughs, William J., Bob Crowder, Ted Robertson, Elanor Vallier-Talbot, and Richard Whitaker. *Weather*. New York: The Nature Company, 1996.
Campbell, Ann-Jeanette, and Ronald Rood. *The New York Public Library Incredible Earth*. New York: Wiley, 1996.
Christian, Spencer. *Can It Really Rain Frogs?* New York: Wiley, 1997.
Darling, Peter. *Crystals*. London: A Quintet Book, 1998.
Deene, Ben. *First Encyclopedia of Seas and Oceans. 2001.* London: Usborne, 2001.
Farndon, John. *How the Earth Works*. Pleasantville, NY: Reader's Digest, 1992.
———. *1000 Facts on Planet Earth*. New York: Barnes and Noble, 2002.
Gibson, Gary. *Science for Fun Experiments*. Brookfield, CT: Copper Beech Books, 1996.
James, Ian. *Planet Earth*. Bath, England: Dempsey Parr, 1998.
Kahl, Jonathan. *Audubon First Field Guide: Weather*. New York: Scholastic, 1998.
Lynch, John. *The Weather*. Toronto: Firefly Books, 2002.
Sherman, Joseph, and Steve Brick. *Energy at Work: Solar Energy*. Mankado, MN: Capstone Press, 2004.
Time-Life Books. *Planet Earth*. Alexandria, Virginia: Time-Life Books, 1997.
VanCleave, Janice. *Janice VanCleave's Energy for Every Kid*. Hoboken, NJ: Wiley, 2005.
———. *Janice VanCleave's Weather*. New York: Wiley, 1995.
Walpole, Brenda. *175 Science Experiments to Amuse and Amaze Your Friends*. New York: Random House, 1988.
Watt, Fiona. *Planet Earth*. London: Usborne, 1991.
Williams, Jack. *The Weather Book*. New York: Vintage Books, 1992.
Wilsdon, Christina. *Audubon First Field Guide: Insects*. New York: Scholastic, 2005.

Engineering

Farndon, John. *1000 Facts on Science and Technology*. New York: Barnes and Noble, 2004.
Harris, David W. *Truss Fun*. Lakewood, CO: BaHa Enterprises, 2000.
Hooker, Saralinda, Christopher Ragus, and Mario G. Salvadori. *The Art of Construction: Projects and Principles for Beginning Engineers and Architects*. Chicago: Chicago Review Press, 1990.
Kaner, Etta. *Bridges*. Toronto: Kids Can Press, 1995.

Kline, Michael P., Carol A. Johmann, and Elizabeth J. Rieth. *Bridges! Amazing Structures to Design, Build & Test*. Charlotte, VT: Williamson Publishing, 1999.

Pollard, Jeanne. *Building Toothpick Bridges*. Chicago: Chicago Review Press, 1990.

General Science

Breckman, Judy. *365 Super Science Experiments*. New York: Sterling Publishing Co., Inc., 2001.

Churchill, Richard E., Louis V. Loeschnig, and Muriel Mandell. *365 Simple Science Experiments with Everyday Materials*. New York: Black Dog and Leventhal Publisher, 1997.

Eyewitness Visual Dictionaries. *The Visual Dictionary of Plants*. New York: Dorling Kindersley, Inc., 1992.

Hann, Judith. *How Science Works*. Pleasantville, New York: Reader's Digest, 1991.

Highlights for Children. *The Highlights Big Book of Science Secrets*. New York: Barnes and Noble, 1997.

Mandell, Muriel. *Simple Science Experiments with Everyday Materials*. New York: Sterling Publishing Co., 1989.

Ontario Science Centre. *Scienceworks: 65 Experiments That Introduce the Fun and Wonder of Science*. Reading, MA: Addison-Wesley Publishing, Inc., 1987.

Reader's Digest. *Did You Know?* Pleasantville, NY: Reader's Digest, 1990.

———. *Why in the World?* Pleasantville, NY: Reader's Digest, 1994.

Robinson, Tom. *The Everything Kids Science Experiment Book*. Avon, MA: Adams Media Corporation, 2001.

Science and Technology Department of the Carnegie Library of Pittsburgh. *The Handy Science Answer Book*. New York: Visible Ink, 1997.

Smith, Alastair, ed. *The Usborne Big Book of Experiments*. New York: Scholastic, 1996.

Stein, Sara. *The Science Book*. New York: Workman Publishing, 1980.

Suplee, Curt. *Everyday Science Explained*. Nashville, Tennessee: National Geographic Society Book Division, 1998.

VanCleave, Janice. *Janice VanCleave's Science Around the World*. Hoboken, NJ: Wiley, 2004.

———. *Janice VanCleave's Super Science Models*. Hoboken, NJ: Wiley, 2004.

———. *Janice VanCleave's 201 Awesome, Magical, Bizarre & Incredible Experiments*. New York: Wiley, 1994.

———. *Janice VanCleave's 202 Oozing, Dripping and Bouncing Experiments*. New York: Wiley, 1996.

———. *Janice VanCleave's 203 Icy, Freezing, Frosty, Cool & Wild Experiments*. New York: Wiley, 1999.

Walpole, Brenda. *175 Science Experiments to Amuse and Amaze Your Friends*. New York: Random House, 1988.

Wollard, Kathy. *How Come?* New York: Workman, 1993.

Physics

Ardley, Neil. *The Science Book of Sound*. New York: Harcourt Brace Jovanovich, 1991.

Franklin, Sharon. *Power Up!* Glenview, IL: GoodYearBooks, 1995.

Gardner, Robert, and Eric Kemer. *Science Projects about Temperature and Heat*. Springfield, NJ: Enslow, 1994.

Glover, David. *Sound and Light*. New York: Kingfisher Books, 1993.

Graham, Ian. *Boats, Ships, Submarines, and Other Floating Machines*. New York: Kingfisher Books, 1993.

Jones, Mary, and Geoff Jones. *Physics*. New York: Cambridge University Press, 1997.

Kentley, Eric. *Boat*. New York: Dorling Kindersley Eyewitness Books, 1992.

Murphy, Pat, Ellen Klages, and Linda Shores. *The Science Explorer*. New York: An Owl Book, 1996.

Potter, Jean. *Science in Seconds with Toys*. New York: Wiley, 1998.

Sabbeth, Alex. *Rubber-band Banjos and Java Jive Bass*. New York: Wiley, 1997.

Seller, Mick. *Sound, Noise, and Music*. New York: Shooting Star Press Inc., 1992.

Soucie Gary. *What's the Difference Between Lenses and Prisms and Other Scientific Things?* New York: Wiley, 1995.

VanCleave, Janice. *Janice VanCleave's Science Through the Ages*. Hoboken, NJ: Wiley, 2002.

———. *Janice VanCleave's Scientists Through the Ages*. Hoboken, NJ: Wiley, 2004.

———. *Physics for Every Kid*. New York: Wiley, 1991.

Wiese, Jim. *Roller Coaster Science*. New York: Wiley, 1994.

Wood, Robert W. *Sound Fundamentals*. New York: Learning Triangle Press, 1997.

Glossary

absorbency The ability of a material to soak up a fluid.
acid A sour-tasting chemical that forms salt and water when mixed with a base.
active solar heating Involves using special devices for absorbing and transporting solar energy.
adhesion The attraction between unlike particles such as particles of water and paper.
agriculture The science that deals with farming concerns.
air The mixture of gases in Earth's atmosphere.
air pressure *See* **atmospheric pressure**.
alviolus An air sac in the lungs; a balloon-shaped structure at the end of each bronchiole.
analyze To examine, compare, and relate all the data.
anatomy The study of the structure of plants; the study of the structure and use of animal body parts.
angular apparent measurement A measurement in degrees of how far or how large objects appear to be.
angular distance The apparent distance measured in degrees.
angular speed Speed measured in degrees per time.
apparent distance In reference to celestial bodies, it is how far apart celestial bodies appear to be from an observer on Earth.
aqueous solution A solution in which water is the solvent.
arc A part of a circle.
artery A blood vessel carrying blood from the heart to the body.
artificial light Light from a man-made source.
asexual reproduction Reproduction involving only one parent.
astronomy The study of celestial bodies.
atmosphere The blanket of gas surrounding a celestial body.
atmospheric pressure The measure of pressure that the atmosphere exerts on surfaces resulting from the collision of gas molecules in Earth's atmosphere; also called air pressure or barometric pressure.
atoms The building blocks of elements.
autumn The climatic season with medium-length cool days; the season following summer and before winter.
auxin A light-sensitive growth chemical.
axis An imaginary line through the center of a body around which the body rotates.
banned Forbidden to be used.
bar graph A graph in which bars are used to show the relationship between two variables.
barometer An instrument used to measure atmospheric pressure.
barometric pressure *See* **atmospheric pressure**.
base A bitter-tasting chemical that forms salt and water when mixed with an acid; metal oxides.
beam bridge The basic bridge design; for example, a log across a creek.
behavior The study of actions that alter the relationship between a plant and its environment; a study in which the actions and reactions of humans and animals are recorded through observational and experimental methods.
biology The study of living things.
blood The liquid in animals that carries nutrients and oxygen to cells and takes away wastes.
blood pressure The force of blood on the walls of arteries.
bob The weight of a pendulum.
bond The force holding chemicals together.
botany The study of plants and plant life.
bronchi Tubes at the end of the trachea that lead to the lungs.
bronchioles Smaller tubes branching from the end of each bronchus.
buoyancy The upward force of a fluid on an object placed in it.
buoyant A measure of how well an object floats.
camouflage A disguise caused by similarities between the color of an animal's body and its environment.
capillary The smallest blood vessels in animals; where oxygen from inhaled air transferred is to the blood and waste from the blood is transferred to the lungs and exhaled.
carbon dioxide (1) A gas used by plants to make food. (2) A gaseous waste in animals.
celestial bodies The natural objects in the sky such as stars, moons, suns, and planets.

celestial motion The study of the motion of celestial bodies.
chemical Any substance with a definite composition made up of one or more elements.
chemical change See **chemical reaction**.
chemical reaction When substances combine or break apart and recombine in a new way to form new substances.
chemical technology engineering The branch of engineering concerned with the application of chemistry in the production of goods and services that humankind considers useful.
chemical weathering The breakdown of crustal materials due to chemical changes of the substances making up the crust.
chemistry The study of what substances are made of and how they change and combine.
chlorophyll A green pigment in plants that captures light so that it can be used in the photosynthesis reaction.
circle graph A graph (also called a pie chart) in which the area of a circle represents a sum of data, and the sizes of the pie-shaped pieces into which the circle is divided represent the amount of data.
climatic seasons Divisions of the year based on average temperature and the amount of time that the Sun is in the sky each day; winter, spring, summer, autumn.
cognitive process The mental process a person uses for remembering, reasoning, understanding, problem solving, evaluating, and using judgment.
cohesion The attraction between like particles such as two water particles.
colorant A substance that selectively absorbs and reflects visible light so that you see a certain color.
colorfastness A measure of how well a dyed material resists fading.
column In reference to a table, it is a vertical listing of data values.
complete fertilizer A fertilizer containing all three primary nutrients: nitrogen (N), phosphorus (P), and potassium (K).
compound A chemical made up of two or more different elements.
compress To press together.
compression (1) A force that pushes the material of a structure together. (2) The part of a longitudinal wave where the particles of the medium are pushed together.
concentrated (1) In reference to a solution, it means to have a large amount of solute. (2) In reference to diffusion, it means particles are grouped together.
concentration The strength of a solution; the amount of solute in a specific amount of solvent.
conclusion A brief summary of what you discovered based on data from your experimental results.
condensation rate The amount of gas that condenses in a certain amount of time.
condense To change from a gas to a liquid state of matter.
control An experiment used for comparison to the results of other experiments.
controlled variables The parts of an experiment that could change but are kept constant.
cotyledon The part of a seed where nutrients are stored.
crust The outer layer of Earth.
crystal The arrangement of particles forming most solids; solids with particles arranged in a regular, repeating pattern with flat surfaces.
crystalline solid A solid made up of crystals.
crystallography The study of the formation of crystals as well as the crystals themselves.
data Recorded collections of information.
date mark A date stamped on the food package with instructions that read "use by date" or "best before date."
decompose To break down into simpler parts; to rot.
degree (°) A unit that can be used to measure all or part of the distance around a circle.
dehydrated Dried out.
density The ratio of mass to volume of an object.
dependent variable The part of an experiment that changes due to changes in the independent variable.
diastolic pressure Blood pressure in the arteries when the heart is resting.
diffusion The movement of particles from one place to another due to a difference in concentration.
dilute Having a low concentration.
dilute solution A solution in which more solute will dissolve at a specific temperature.
displace To push aside.
displacement In reference to a pendulum, it is the distance that it moves to one side from its vertical position.
dissolved In reference to a solute, it means to be separated into parts and spread throughout.
dye A substance that contains a colorant dissolved in a liquid.
Earth science The study of the parts of Earth: the **atmosphere** (the gas layer surrounding Earth), the **lithosphere** (the outer solid parts), and the **hydrosphere** (the water parts).

ecology The study of relationships of living things to other living things and to their environment.

elements Basic chemical substances; substances that contain only one kind of atom and that cannot be broken down into simpler substances.

embryo An organism's earliest stage of development.

energy The capacity to make things change.

engineering The study of applying scientific knowledge for practical purposes.

entomology The study of insects.

epithelial cells Cells on the surface of organisms.

equator In reference to Earth, it is an imaginary line dividing Earth in half.

erosion The process by which rocks and other materials of Earth's crust are broken down and carried away by natural agents such as water, ice, and gravity.

evaporate To change from a liquid to a gas.

evaporation The process by which a liquid changes into a gas.

evaporation rate The amount of liquid that evaporates in a certain amount of time.

exhale To breathe out.

experimental data Observations and/or measured facts obtained from a project experiment.

expiration date The date on food that indicates when you can expect it to go bad.

exploratory experiment An experiment in which the results are part of the project research.

face The flat surface of a solid.

fade To become lighter in color.

fertilizer A soil additive containing plant nutrients that promote plant growth.

flexible Able to change shape in response to a force, then recover the original shape when the force is removed.

fluid A liquid or a gas.

food science The study of food, including the causes of food deterioration and the nature of food, such as nutritional value.

food technology engineering The branch of engineering concerned with the application of food science to the selection, preservation, processing, packaging, and distribution of safe, nutritious, and wholesome food.

force A push or pull on an object.

frequency The number of vibrations per second.

fungus A single-celled or multicellular organism that obtains food by the direct absorption of nutrients.

gas A state of matter that has no definite shape or volume.

gel A semisolid formed by gelling.

gelatin An animal protein produced by boiling animal parts in water; an odorless, tasteless, and colorless substance that forms a gel when dissolved into hot water and then cooled.

gelling The process by which a gel is formed by mixing gelatin with hot water, then allowing it to cool.

geotropism Plant movement due to growth in response to gravity.

germination The sprouting of seeds.

germination starting time (GST) The time it takes from planting a seed to the first signs of growth.

germination time (GT) The time it takes from planting a seed to the end of germination; determined by the time it takes for the epicotyl to fully emerge from the cotyledons.

glucose A type of sugar produced by plants. It is needed by both plants and animals for energy.

gnomon The part of a sundial that casts a shadow on the scaled surface of the sundial.

graph A visual representation of data that shows a relationship between two variables.

gravity The force pulling objects toward the center of Earth; gravity increases as the mass of an object increases.

guard cells Cells that open and close stomata.

heat The energy that flows from a warm material to a cool material.

herbicide A pesticide for weeds.

heterogeneous mixture A mixture that is not the same throughout.

homogeneous mixture A mixture that has the same composition throughout.

horizon Where the sky appears to touch Earth.

humidity The measure of the amount of water vapor in air.

hydrometer An instrument used to measure the specific gravity of a liquid.

hydrosphere The part of Earth that is water.

hypertension A condition resulting from blood pressure being consistently higher than normal during rest time.

hypha (pl. hyphae) Threadlike structure forming mycelia.

independent variable The part of an experiment that is purposely changed.

inhale To breathe in.

inhibition The stopping of one brain process in order for another response to be processed.

inquiry questions Questions about a science topic that may or may not be used as the project problem.

insecticide A pesticide for insects.

insect pest management The study of methods of controlling insects that affect crop production as well as the health of farm animals.

interference In reference to memory, it is one of the reasons that short-term information is forgotten; information in storage is distorted as new information is stored.

interpret In reference to data, it means to explain by restating the data.

introduction The part of a report that contains a statement of your purpose, along with some of the background information that led you to make the study and what you hoped to achieve from it.

invertebrate An animal without a backbone.

lateral force A force directed at the side of a structure.

line graph A graph in which one or more lines are used to show the relationship between the two quantitative variables.

liquid A state of matter with a definite volume but no definite shape.

lithosphere The part of Earth that is solid.

log book A science diary or journal, which is a written record of your science project from start to finish.

longevity A measure of the length of life.

longitudinal waves Waves that have areas of compression and rarefraction.

long-term memory Information that you can recall after days and even years.

lungs Balloonlike structures in the chest that are used to exchange oxygen and carbon dioxide between your blood and the atmosphere.

mass The amount of material in an object.

mathematics The use of numbers and symbols to study amounts and forms.

matter The substance from which all objects are made; anything that has mass and takes up space.

mechanical weathering The breakdown of crustal material by physical means.

mechanics The study of objects in motion and the forces that produce the motion.

medium Any solid, liquid, or gas; a substance through which sound can travel.

melting The process of changing from a solid to a liquid state of matter.

membrane A thin sheet of flexible material.

memory The ability to retain and recall past experiences.

meteorology The study of weather, climate, and Earth's atmosphere.

microbe An organism too small to be seen with the unaided eye.

microbiology The study of microscopic organisms such as fungi, bacteria, and protista.

microscopic level The level at which particles are so small that they cannot be seen except by magnification, such as with a microscope.

microscopic organism An organism that you need a microscope to see because it is so small.

microwave A form of electromagnetic radiation.

mixture Two or more substances mixed together.

mold A fungus that produces a fuzzy, cobweblike growth on moist materials, including food.

mordant A chemical that bonds the colorant in a dye to a material.

mycelium (pl. mycelia) A fungal body made of a netlike mass of hyphae.

natural satellite A celestial body orbiting another; Earth's moon.

negative tropism The movement of an organism away from the stimuli.

nerve A special fiber that transports impulses between the brain and body; made of bundles of thousands of neurons.

nerve impulse An electric signal traveling from one neuron to another.

net force The sum of all forces simultaneously acting on an object.

neuron A nerve cell.

neutral Neither an acid nor a base.

Northern Hemisphere In reference to Earth, it is the part north of the equator.

nutrient A nourishing material necessary for life and growth.

observation Information collected about something by using your senses.

oceanography The study of the oceans and marine organisms.

organic Made from living material.

organic pesticide A pesticide that comes from natural sources, including plants such as marigolds, and minerals such as boric acid.

oxidation A chemical reaction in which one chemical combines with oxygen.

passive solar heating Solar heating that does not use any mechanical means of distributing the collected heat; instead, it is direct heating from sunlight.

pendulum A weight hung so that it swings about a pivot.

percussion instrument A musical instrument that makes sounds when it is struck or shaken.

period (T) In reference to a pendulum, it is the time required to complete one vibration.

periodic motion Any type of motion that successively repeats itself in equal intervals of time.

permeability The ability of a material to allow substances to diffuse through it.

pest An unwanted organism.

pesticide A substance intended to repel, kill, or control any kind of pest.
pharynx The throat.
photosynthesis A process in plants in which light energy is used to change carbon dioxide and water into glucose and water.
phototropism The movement of organisms in response to light.
pH scale The scale for measuring the strength of an acid or a base.
physical change A change in the appearance of matter, but its properties and makeup remain the same.
physics The study of forms of energy and the laws of motion.
physiography The study of the physical features of Earth's surface.
physiology The study of life processes of plants and animals.
pigment A substance that provides color to a material.
pitch In reference to sound, it is how the frequency of a sound is perceived by the brain; the greater the frequency, the higher the pitch.
pivot The point on which something turns.
positive tropism The movement of an organism toward the stimuli.
precipitate To separate a solid from a solution.
predator An animal that kills and eats other animals.
primary nutrient The nutrient most often lacking in soil; nitrogen, phosphorus, and potassium.
primary research Research you collect on your own.
product A chemical produced in a chemical reaction.
product development engineering The branch of engineering concerned with designing, developing, and testing new products.
project abstract A brief overview of a scientific project.
project category A group of related science topics.
project conclusion A summary of the results of the project experiment and a statement of how the results relate to the hypothesis.
project display A visual representation of all the work that you have done.
project experiment An experiment designed to test the hypothesis of a science project; a test to determine a relationship between two variables: an independent variable and a dependent variable.
project hypothesis An idea about the solution to a problem based on knowledge and research.

project problem A scientific question or purpose for a science project.
project report A written report of an entire project from start to finish.
project research An in-depth study of the project topic with the objective of expressing a project problem, proposing a hypothesis, and designing a project experiment to test the hypothesis.
project summaries The project abstract and project report.
project title A descriptive heading for a project.
protective coloration The coloring that helps to camouflage an animal from a predator.
protein A substance in living organisms necessary for their survival and growth; a large particle make of one or more chemical chains.
qualitative observation A description of the physical properties of something.
quantitative observation A description of the amount of something.
radiant energy Energy in the form of waves that can travel through space; also called radiation.
rarefaction (1) The force that pulls the material of a structure apart. (2) The part of a longitudinal wave where particles of the medium are spread apart.
ratio A pair of numbers used to compare quantities.
raw data Data collected as a result of observing experimental results.
reactant A starting chemical that is changed during a chemical reaction.
refrigerant A material used to cool other materials.
regeneration The growth of new tissue or parts of an organism that have been lost or destroyed.
reproduction The process of producing a new organism.
research The process of collecting information.
revolve To move in a curved path around another object.
root system The parts of a plant that generally grow below ground; the parts of a plant that anchor it in the ground and take in water and nutrients from the soil.
rotate To turn on an axis.
row In reference to a table, it is a horizontal listing of data values.
salinity The salt concentration in a salt and water solution.
sap In plants, it is the solution of water and other nutrients.
saturated solution A solution in which the maximum amount of solute is dissolved in a solvent at a given temperature.

science A system of knowledge about the nature of things in the universe.
science fair An organized contest in which science projects are compared and judged based on predetermined criteria.
science problem A science question or purpose.
science project An investigation that is designed to find the answer to one specific science problem.
secondary nutrients Three of the thirteen necessary elemental plant nutrients generally found in soils: calcium (Ca), magnesium (Mg), and sulfur (S).
secondary research Information and/or data that someone else has collected such as that found in books, magazines, and electronic sources.
semipermeable The ability of a material to allow some particles to pass through but not others.
sensory information Information collected by hearing, seeing, touching, tasting, and smelling.
sensory memory The ability to retain impressions of sensory information after the original stimulus has ceased; this memory is thought to last from 1 second to 2 seconds.
sexual reproduction Reproduction involving two parents.
shelf life The period during which food may be stored and remain suitable and safe to eat.
shoot system The part of a plant that generally grows above ground.
short-term memory Your working memory; your primary memory or active memory, the one you use most of the time.
solar energy A form of radiant energy that comes from the Sun.
solar heating A process of using solar energy to heat materials. *See also* **active solar heating**; **passive solar heating**.
solid A state of matter that has a definite shape and volume.
solute The part of a solution being dissolved.
solution A mixture of a liquid with substances dissolved in it; a homogeneous mixture of a solute and a solvent.
solvent The part of a solution doing the dissolving.
sound Energy in the form of waves produced by vibrating material that can only travel through a medium; energy produced by vibrating material that can be heard; also called **sound waves**.
sound waves Waves produced as a result of the vibration of a material.
specific gravity The ratio of the density of a material to the density of water.
specific heat A measure of how well a material resists changing its temperature.
speed A measurement of distance in a given time period.
spore A reproductive cell.
spring The climatic season following winter with medium-length cool days.
sprout To begin to grow.
stale A decrease in the quality of a food's taste due to age.
states of matter Solid, liquid, and gas.
stellar science The study of stars including their composition, magnitude, classification, structure, and groupings.
stimulus (pl. **stimuli**) Something that tempo rarily excites or quickens a response in an organism.
stomata Special openings in the outer layer of plants, generally in the leaves, through which gases can pass.
Stroop test A test that demonstrates the interference that happens in the brain when two simultaneous thinking process are involved such as reading words and identifying colors.
structural engineering The branch of engineering concerned with designing as well as testing the strength of structures including bridges and dams.
sublimation The change from a solid to a gas or vice versa.
summer The climatic season with the longest and hottest days.
summer solstice The first day of summer on or about June 21/June 22 in the Northern Hemisphere when the Sun's zenith is highest during the year.
sundial One of the oldest, if not the oldest, known device for the measurement of time.
surface area The size of the surface of an object.
suspension A liquid mixture made of parts that separate upon standing.
system Different parts working together as one unit.
systolic pressure The blood pressure on the inside walls of arteries when the heart contracts and pushes blood out.
table A chart in which data is presented in rows and columns.
table of contents The second page of a report containing a list of everything in the report including a page number for the beginning of each section.
tarnish Any coating on a metal that discolors and/or dulls its shiny surface.
taste buds Special cells on your tongue and on the roof and the back of your mouth that detect taste.

temperature A measure of how hot or cold a material is.
tension A force that pulls materials apart.
texture How a surface feels.
thixotropic liquid A liquid whose viscosity decreases with motion.
tidal air The amount of air involved during normal, relaxed inhaling and exhaling.
title A descriptive heading.
title page The first page of a report with the project title centered on the page and your name, school, and grade in the lower right-hand corner.
topic research Research done with the objective of selecting a science project topic.
trace elements Seven of the thirteen necessary elemental plant nutrients needed in only very small amount: boron (B), copper (Cu), iron (Fe), chloride (Cl), manganese (Mn), molybdenum (Mo), and zinc (Zn).
trachea A breathing tube.
transpiration The process by which plants lose water through stomata.
transpiration rate The amount of water lost by a plant in a specific period of time.
tropism The movement of an organism in response to a stimulus. *See also* **negative tropism**; **positive tropism**.
truss A simple skeletal structure made up of straight beams forming triangular shapes.
truss bridge A bridge with trusses.
turgor The pressure within plant cells.
unit cells The smallest group of particles within a crystal that retain the geometric shape of the crystal.
unsaturated solution A solution with less than the maximum amount of solute.
vapor The gaseous state of a substance at a temperature at which the substance is usually in a solid or liquid state.

vaporize The change from a liquid to the gas state of matter.
variables Things that can change.
vascular plant A plant that contains tubelike structures that transport nutrients throughout the plant.
vibrate To move back and forth.
vibration A back-and-forth or up-and-down motion.
visible light Light the human eye can see.
visible spectrum A list of visible light in order from least to most energy: red, yellow, orange, green, blue, indigo, and violet.
vital capacity The largest amount of air that can be exhaled after taking a deep breath.
volume The amount of space an object takes up.
weather Conditions in the atmosphere.
weathering The part of erosion that involves only the breakdown of crustal materials.
weight The measure of gravity on an object; weight increases with mass.
white light A combination of all light colors in the visible spectrum.
wilt To become limp or droopy.
winter The climatic season that has the shortest and coldest days; it starts at winter solstice.
winter solstice The first day of winter on or about December 21/December 22 in the Northern Hemisphere when the Sun's zenith is lowest during the year.
work The transfer of energy when a force causes an object to move.
***x*-axis** The horizontal axis on a line graph.
xylem Tubelike structures that transport water and nutrients in the soil throughout vascular plants.
***y*-axis** The vertical axis on a line graph.
zoology The study of animals and animal life.

Index

absorbency, 12, 92, 126
acid, 81, 126
active solar heating, 108, 126
adhesion, 92, 126
agriculture, 9, 126
  project ideas, 117
  projects, 36–39
air, 84, 126
air pressure. *See* atmospheric pressure
alviolus, 63, 126
analyze, 22, 126
anatomy, 9, 10, 126
angular apparent measurement, 10, 126
angular distance, 100, 126
angular speed, 100, 126
ants, 38–39
apparent distance, 100, 126
aqueous solution, 74, 126
arc, 114, 126
arteries, 71, 126
artificial light, 48, 126
asexual reproduction, 60, 126
Aspergillus niger, 58
astronomy, 9, 126
  projects, 40–43
atmosphere, 10, 84, 126
atmospheric pressure, 84, 126
atoms, 10, 126
autumn, 55, 126
auxin, 47, 126
axis, 40, 42, 126

banned, 38, 126
bar graph, 22, 126
barometer, 84, 126
barometric pressure. *See* atmospheric pressure
base, 81, 126
beam bridge, 99, 126
behavior, 9, 126
bibliography, 16
biology, 9, 10, 126
  project ideas, 117–118

projects, 44–71
blood, 62, 126
blood pressure, 70–71
  definition of, 70, 126
  diastolic pressure, 70, 126
  hypertension, 70, 128
  systolic pressure, 70, 131
bob, 114, 126
bonds, 56, 126
botany, 9, 126
bread mold, 58–59
bridge:
  beam bridge, 99, 126
  strength, 98–99
  truss bridge, 98–99, 132
bronchi, 62, 126
bronchioles, 62, 126
buoyancy, 112–113
  definition, 11, 112, 126
buoyant, 112, 126

calcium propionate, 58–59
camouflage, 54–55
  definition of, 54, 126
  protective coloration, 54, 130
capillary, 64, 130
carbon dioxide, 44, 62, 126
celestial bodies, 9, 100, 126
celestial motion, 9, 127
chemical, 10, 80, 127
chemical changes, 10, 80, 127
chemical reaction, 80, 127
chemical technology engineering, 10, 127
chemical weathering, 90, 127
chemistry, 10, 127
  project ideas, 118–119
  projects, 72–83
chlorophyll, 48, 55, 127
circle graph, 22–23
  definition of, 22, 127
climatic seasons:
  autumn, 55, 126
  definition, 54, 127
  spring, 54, 131

summer, 54, 131
winter, 54, 132
cognitive process, 66, 131
cohesion, 92, 131
colorant, 82, 127
colorfastness, 82, 127
column, 21, 127
complete fertilizer, 36, 127
compound, 80, 127
compress, 76, 127
compression, 110, 127
concentrated, 96, 127
concentration, 74, 96, 127
conclusion, 2, 28, 127
condensation rate, 86–87, 127
condense, 86, 127
control:
  definition of, 3, 19, 127
  example, 19
controlled variable, 3, 19, 127
cotyledon, 50, 127
crust, 90, 127
crystal, 76, 127
crystalline solid, 76, 127
crystallography, 10, 127

data:
  definition of, 2, 127
  project, 8
  raw, 2, 130
date mark, 94, 127
DDT, 38
degree, 42, 127
dehydrated, 94, 127
density, 88, 127
dependent variable, 3, 17, 19, 127
diastolic pressure, 70, 126
diffusion, 96, 126
dilute, 74, 127
displacement, 114, 127
displaces, 112, 127
dye, 82, 127

Earth science, 10, 128
  project ideas, 119

Earth science (*continued*)
   projects, 84–91
Earth's natural satellite, 9, 42–43
ecology, 9, 128
elements:
   definition of, 36, 80, 128
   trace, 36, 132
embryo, 50, 128
energy, 11, 128
engineering, 10, 128
   project ideas, 119–120
   projects, 92–99
entomology, 14, 128
epithelial cells, 60, 128
equator, 41, 128
erosion, 90–91
   definition of, 90, 128
evaporation, 73, 128
evaporation rate, 73, 86, 128
exhale, 62, 128
experimental data. *See* raw data
expiration date, 94, 128
exploratory experiment, 2, 128

face, 77, 128
fade, 82, 128
fertilizer, 36–37
   complete, 36, 127
   definition of, 36, 128
flexible, 56, 128
flowers:
   longevity of, 44–45
   sap, 44, 131
fluid, 10, 128
food science:
   definition of, 9, 128
   food freshness, 94–97
food technology engineering:
   definition of, 10, 128
   food freshness, 94–97
force:
   compression, 98, 127
   definition of, 11, 98, 128
   gravity, 98, 128
   lateral, 98, 129
   tension, 98, 132
   weight, 98, 132
frequency, 110, 128
fungus, 58, 128

gas, 72, 128

gel:
   definition of, 56, 128
   flexibility of, 56–57
gelatin, 56, 128
gelling, 56, 128
geotropism, 9, 128
germination, 50–51
   definition of, 50, 128
germination starting time (GST), 51, 128
germination time, 51, 128
glucose:
   definition of, 44, 128
   effect on cut flowers, 44–45
gnomon, 40, 128
graph:
   bar graph, 22, 126
   circle graph, 22, 127
   definition of, 22, 128
   line graph, 24, 129
gravity, 98, 128
guard cells, 52, 129

hand measurements, 100–101
heat, 11, 104, 106, 128
herbicide, 38, 128
heterogeneous mixture, 78–79
   definition of, 10, 78, 128
homogeneous mixture, 10, 128
horizon, 43, 128
humidity, 87, 128
hydrometer:
   definition of, 88, 128
   homemade, 89
hydrosphere, 10, 128
hypertension, 70, 128
hypha, 58, 128

independent variable, 3, 19, 129
inhale, 62, 128
inhibition, 65, 129
inquiry questions, 12, 128
insecticide, 38–39
   definition of, 38, 128
insect pest management, 9, 129
interference, 66, 129
interpret, 22, 129
introduction, 26–27, 129
invertebrates, 60, 129

ketchup:

   thickness of, 78–79
lateral force, 98, 129
light:
   artificial light, 48, 126
   effect on plants, 46–49
   visible, 46, 132
   white, 46, 132
line graph, 24, 129
liquid, 72, 129
lithosphere, 10, 129
log book, 7–11
   definition of, 1, 129
longevity:
   definition of, 44, 129
   flower, 44–45
longitudinal wave, 104, 129
long-term memory, 66, 129
lungs:
   capacity of, 62–63
   definition of, 62, 129

Man in the Moon, 42–43
mass, 72, 129
mathematics, 11, 129
   project ideas, 120
   projects, 100–103
matter, 72, 129
mechanical weathering, 90, 129
mechanics, 104, 129
medium, 11, 110, 129
melting, 73, 129
membrane, 96, 129
memory:
   definition of, 66, 129
   long-term, 66, 129
   short-term, 66, 131
meteorology, 10, 129
microbe, 44, 129
microbiology, 9, 129
microscopic level, 76, 129
microscopic organisms, 9, 129
microwave:
   definition of, 51, 129
   effect on seeds, 50–51
mixture:
   definition of, 10, 129
   dyes, 102–103
   heterogeneous mixture, 10, 78–79, 128
   homogeneous mixture, 10, 128
   suspension, 91, 131
mold, 58, 129

Moon, 9, 42–43
mordant, 83, 128
mycelium, 58, 129

natural satellite, 9, 100, 129
negative tropism, 46, 129
net force, 114, 129
neutral, 81, 129
Northern Hemisphere, 41, 129
nutrients:
   definition of, 9, 36, 129
   primary, 36, 130
   secondary, 36, 131

observations:
   definition of, 21, 129
   qualitative, 21, 130
   quantitative, 21, 130
oceanography, 10, 129
organic pesticide, 38, 129
oxidation, 80, 129

paper:
   absorbency, 10, 92, 126
   printing quality, 92–93
passive solar heating, 108–109
   definition of, 108, 130
pendulum, 114–115
   bob, 115, 126
   definition of, 114, 130
   displacement, 114, 127
   period, 114, 130
   pivot, 114, 130
percussion instrument, 111, 130
period (T), 114, 130
periodic motion, 11, 130
permeability, 96, 137
pest, 38, 129
pesticide:
   banned, 38, 126
   definition of, 38, 130
   herbicide, 38, 128
   insecticide, 38, 129
   organic, 38, 129
pharynx, 62, 130
photosynthesis, 44, 48, 130
phototropism, 46–47
   definition of, 9, 130
   effect of the color of light, 46–47
pH scale, 81, 130
physical changes, 10, 130

physics, 11, 130
   project ideas, 120–121
   projects, 104–115
physiography, 9, 130
physiology, 9, 10, 130
pie chart. *See* circle graph
pigment, 55, 130
pitch, 110, 130
pivot, 114, 130
planaria, 60
plant:
   growth, 48–49
   leaves, 52–53
   seeds, 50–51
   transpiration, 52–53, 132
plastic food wrap:
   food freshness, 96–99
positive tropism, 46, 130
precipitating, 77, 132
predator, 54, 130
primary nutrient, 36, 130
primary research, 14–15
   definition of, 14, 130
product, 80, 130
product development engineering, 10, 130
project abstract, 2, 130
project acknowledgments, 28–29
project calendar, 7
project category, 9–11
   definition of, 1, 130
project conclusion, 2, 28, 127
project data, 8, 21–24
project discussion, 28
project display, 8, 30–32
   definition of, 2, 130
project evaluation, 33–34
project experiment, 8, 19–20, 27–28
   definition of, 2, 17, 19, 130
project hypothesis, 8, 18
   definition of, 2, 130
   examples, 18
project oral presentation and evaluation, 8, 33–34
project problem, 8, 17
   definition of, 2, 130
project references, 29
project report, 8, 26–27
   definition of, 2, 26, 130
project research, 14–16
   definition of, 2, 130
   exploratory experiment, 2, 128

primary research, 14–15, 129
secondary research, 15–16, 130
project summaries, 8, 25–29
   abstract, 25, 130
   report, 2, 26, 130
project title, 25, 130
project topic research. *See* topic research
protective coloration, 54, 130
protein, 56, 130

qualitative observations, 21, 130
quantitative observations, 21, 130

radiant energy:
   definition of, 11, 46, 51, 108, 128
   light, 44, 46, 108,
   microwave, 51, 129
   solar energy, 108–109
rarefaction, 110, 129
ratio, 102–103
   definition of, 10, 102, 130
raw data, 21–24
   definition of, 2, 21, 130
reactant, 80, 130
refrigerant, 104–105
   definition of, 104, 130
   surface area, 104–105
regeneration, 60–61, 130
reproduction, 10, 130
research:
   definition of, 1, 130
   primary, 14, 130
   project research, 2, 14–16, 130
   secondary, 15, 131
   topic research, 1, 12–13, 132
respiration rate, 17
revolve, 41, 132
root system, 50, 132
rotation:
   Earth's, 40–43
   definition of, 40, 42, 130
row, 21, 130

salinity, 88–89
   definition of, 88, 130
   ocean, 88–89
   parts per thousand, 88
sap, 44, 130
satellite, 100
saturated solution, 75, 130

saturated solution (*continued*)
   effect of temperature on
      preparing, 74–75
science, 1, 131
science fair, 1, 131
science problem, 1, 131
science project, 1, 131
secondary nutrients, 36, 131
secondary research, 15–16
   definition of, 15, 131
seed:
   effect of microwaves on, 50–51
   germination, 50–51, 128
   germination starting time, 51, 128
   germination time, 51, 128
semipermeable, 96, 131
sensory information, 66, 131
sensory memory, 66, 131
sensory receptors, 131
sexual reproduction, 10, 131
shelf life, 94–95
   date mark, 94, 127
   definition of, 94, 131
   expiration date, 94, 128
shoot system, 50, 131
short-term memory: 66–67
   definition of, 66, 131
solar, 108, 131
solar energy, 108, 131
solar heating:
   active, 108, 127
   definition of, 108, 131
   passive, 108–109, 129
solid, 72, 131
solute, 74, 131
solutions:
   aqueous, 74, 126
   definition of, 10, 44, 74, 131
   sap, 44, 131
   saturated, 75, 130
   unsaturated, 75, 132
solvent, 74, 131
sound,
   definition of, 11, 110, 131
sound waves. *See* sound
specific gravity:
   definition of, 88, 131
   water, 88
specific heat, 106–107
   definition of, 106, 131

speed:
   angular speed, 100–101, 126
   definition of, 101, 131
   Moon, 100–101
spore, 58, 131
spring, 54, 131
sprout, 50, 131
stale, 94, 131
states of matter:
   definition of, 10, 72, 131
   gas, 72, 128
   liquid, 72, 129
   solid, 72, 131
stellar science, 9, 131
stimulus:
   definition of, 9, 46, 131
   light, 46–47
stomata, 52, 131
Stroop test, 64–65, 131
structural engineering, 10, 131
sublimation, 13, 131
summer, 54, 131
summer solstice, 41, 131
sundial, 40, 131
surface area, 104, 131
suspension, 91, 131
system, 98, 131
   root system, 50, 130
   shoot system, 50, 131
systolic pressure, 70, 131

table, 21, 131
table of contents, project report, 26, 131
tarnish, 80–81, 131
taste, 68–69
taste buds, 67, 131
temperature, 75, 86, 104, 131
texture, 92, 132
thixotropic liquid, 78–79
   definition of, 78, 131
tidal air, 63, 132
title, 21, 132
title page, 132
topic research, 12–13
   definition of, 1, 12, 132
   log book, 7–8
trace elements, 36, 132
trachea, 62, 132
transpiration, 52–53
   definition of, 9, 52, 132

   rate of, 52, 132
tropism:
   definition of, 9, 132
   geotropism, 9, 128
   negative tropism, 46, 129
   phototropism, 9, 46–47, 130
   positive tropism, 46, 130
truss, 99, 132
truss bridge, 98–99
   definition of, 99, 132
turgor, 52, 132

unit cell, 76, 132
unsaturated solution, 75, 132

vapor, 73, 132
vaporize, 13, 52, 73, 132
variable:
   controlled, 3, 19, 127
   definition of, 3, 132
   dependent, 3, 19, 127
   independent, 3, 19, 129
vascular plants, 37, 132
vibration, 11, 76, 110, 132
visible light, 46, 82, 132
visible spectrum, 46, 82, 132
vital capacity, 63, 132
volume, 72, 132

weather:
   definition of, 84, 132
   predicting, 84–85
weathering:
   chemical, 90, 127
   definition of, 90, 132
   mechanical, 90, 129
weight, 98, 132
white light, 46, 82, 132
wilt:
   definition of, 44, 52, 132
   flowers, 44
winter, 54, 132
winter solstice, 41, 132
work, 11, 132

x-axis, 24, 132
xylem, 37, 132

y-axis, 24, 132

zoology, 10, 132

APR 11 2008
25⁰⁵